ALTRUISTIC
SERVICE LEADERSHIP

ALTRUISTIC SERVICE LEADERSHIP

Prophet Muhammad's Leadership

The Paragon of Excellence

ISMAIL NOOR

PARTRIDGE
A Penguin Random House Company

To order additional copies of this book, contact
Toll Free 800 101 2657 (Singapore)
Toll Free 1 800 81 7340 (Malaysia)
orders.singapore@partridgepublishing.com

www.partridgepublishing.com/singapore

Contents

UNIVERSITI SAINS MALAYSIA

FOREWORD

The world is in multiple crises. Economies have been devastated by financial debacles. The ecology of the planet is in a dangerous state with many indicators on the verge of tipping points, if not already past them. The global governance order is in a moral crisis with double standards galore and hypocrisy dominating the big picture.

Sadly, the world is driven by greed and violence, and by manipulation and waste. It is also an unhappy world. The World Health Organization (WHO) once estimated that one person commits suicide every 40 seconds, and one person is killed in war zones every 100 seconds. The horror and terror is that those killed are mostly civilians, many of them women and children.

Most of all, there is a global crisis in leadership. We need leaders everywhere who embody peace and justice, care and compassion. We need leadership based on knowledge and integrity, principled action and dedicated competence. The Prophet Muhammad *s.a.w.* provided us with such leadership and the world needs to learn from his struggles and his journey.

This very unique guidebook, in the form of a practical manual by an outstanding Malaysian scholar, educator and motivator – Dr Ismail Noor - could not have been more timely. This remarkable book systematically enables us to emulate the Prophet's values and practices that not only make for good governance, but can be a source of inspiration for us all. He shares with us the Prophet's struggles and knowledge, wisdom and compassion through the many concrete lessons for making a better world. The book is brilliantly organized and systematically synthesized into a series of modules that can be the basis for the transformational change the world so badly needs.

My hope is that this great book is read and practiced by many and I also hope that it gets translated into as many languages of the world.

Professor Dato' Anwar Fazal
Director, Right Livelihood College
Penang, Malaysia
8 February, 2011

Professor Dato' (Dr) Anwar Fazal
Director, Right Livelihood College
Universiti Sains Malaysia
Penang
Malaysia

DEDICATION

In the name of our Creator, **Allah SWT**, may it please Him that I express my appreciation to the Right Honourable Tun Abdullah Ahmad Badawi, Malaysia's fifth prime minister, who first honoured me by launching the first edition of this book in 1998. The book is now in its second revised edition, bearing the title **Altruistic Service Leadership**, which appropriately describes the personal leadership style of Muhammad *s.a.w.*, the Prophet of Islam.

[Note: from here on, whenever the name of Allah is written it should be verbally affixed with the mention of *Subhanahu-wa-Taala* (*SWT*) and when the Prophet's name is mentioned, it should be verbally affixed with the mention of *salallahu-alaihi-wassalam* (*s.a.w*). in its Arabic entirety after the name is mentioned].

This book is also humbly dedicated to my late parents Haji Mohamed Noor bin Ismail and Hajah Ramlah binti Abdul Rahman, who had in their lifetime provided me the lifeline and inspiration to see the efforts of my work come to fruition.

And to my beloved wife Hajah Marina binti Abdullah and my daughter Elina Noor binti Ismail, an Oxford Law graduate who have continually inspired me in the editing and continued review of the manuscript.

ACKNOWLEDGEMENT

I would like to express my sincerest gratitude to my friends Dr Syed Omar Sharifuddin Syed Ikhsan of the Malaysian Government's National Institute of Public Administration (INTAN) and Datuk (Dr) Anwar Fazal, then a visiting professor at the Universiti Sains Malaysia in Penang, for their unstinting support in the propagation of the holistic message of this guidebook; also to Professor Dr Md Golam Mohiuddin of the Islamic University, Kushtia, Bangladesh, who has included extracts of my earlier edition in his well-researched book titled 'Islamic Management'. My thanks also to Dr Ramazan Altinok, then Head of E-Government Advisory Group of the Republic of Turkey who had in mind to translate my book into the Turkish and Arabic languages. On this, I would like to thank my adviser, best-selling author Ustaz Shamsul bin Mohd Nor, and Brig. Gen. (R) Dato' Abdul Rahim bin Abdul Rahman, for encouraging me to forge ahead with the purpose of passing the message of the Prophet's leadership to the younger generation into the international arena.

Remembering also the support given by academic and training institutions like the Universiti Putra Malaysia (UPM), University of Malaya (UM), the International Islamic University of Malaysia (IIUM), the Universiti Teknologi MARA (UiTM), and the National Institute of Public Administration (INTAN) Malaysia, whose respective faculties and departments had in the past supported my work by positively critiquing and suggesting improvements to my writing for the purpose of a better outreach and outcome – to them I would like to put on record here my wholehearted appreciation.

Bismillahhirrahmaanirrahiim

O you who believe!
Obey Allah, and obey His Messenger
And those who are in authority among you
And if you differ in anything among yourselves
Refer it to Allah and His Messenger –
If you are believers in Allah and the Last Day
That is the best and most commendable

[Al-Qur'an, Surah An-Nisaa, Women: 4:59]

THIS GUIDEBOOK

THE SCOPE

This guidebook is intended to cover the profile, roles and functions of the Prophet Muhammad in the major areas and thrusts of his documented life history. It attempts to provide an insight into the Prophet's life, particularly since the attainment of divine prophethood status, in the varied critical areas of his personal, societal, and holistic development, all in the cause of the Creator, Allah *SWT*, as:

- A Visionary to a Transformational Leader
- Head of an Extended Family
- A Manager-Administrator
- A Strategic Military Commander
- A Judge and Arbitrator
- A Social Entrepreneur
- A Ruler, Diplomat and Statesman
- A Mentor Team Leader
- The Eternal Messenger

Discussions into the roles and functions of the Prophet Muhammad *s.a.w* are dealt with judiciously on a cross-comparative basis with some modern leadership concepts. Each chapter can represent a training module, which can appropriately be accompanied by selected critical incidents, simulations and/or group or personal exercises. The aim is to mentally stimulate and physiologically enthuse the participants into interactive mode so as to progressively enhance the learning process through experiential learning.

This guidebook is deemed essential for all Muslim managers, not just for those who manage the training or human resource development function in organizations, but also for all managers – the rationale being that every single manager performs the role of people developer. It does not, however, preclude non-Muslims from using it because the Holy Qu'ran exhorts its central, universal message to all of mankind.

Leadership is a human facet that should be handled with a great sense of trust and humility, the trust from God Almighty to prosper the earth we live on and the trust the comes from people of all races, religion, creed and culture. The Prophet of Islam was the embodiment of this trust and humility that with the power he wielded, he did not succumb to the corruption, multiple sins or even misdemeanours of his era. Such a leadership model is certainly worth emulating for all times.

PREFACE

I was performing my *Hajj* obligation in Mecca (from here on spelt Makkah) in 1997, when in between daily obligatory prayers, as I sat leaning against a pillar, reading (an excellent book titled, *"The Last Messenger With A Lasting Message"* by Ziauddin Kirmani) and writing some judicious notes in the great holy mosque – Masjid Al-Haram – when suddenly someone who introduced himself as a professor from a Bangladesh agricultural university came by and sat next to me casually interjecting, "Brother, I see you are reading and taking notes on the biography of our Prophet..." and after some small talk he said, "May I urge you to write and publish a book on the Prophet's leadership?" I felt his unexpected intervention was like a bolt from the blue.

Nevertheless, that night in my room at the old Hotel Makkah, I thought about the good professor's challenge to me, and *voilà* after a full year's concerted effort and with the help of the then Bank Islam Research & Training Institute (BIRT) in Kuala Lumpur, I had successfully completed the writing of the first edition of a basic leadership and management training guidebook bearing the title, "PROPHET MUHAMMAD'S LEADERSHIP".

It was a truly worthwhile endeavour, more so because I had also field-tested the draft manuscript for constructive feedback and comments at the International Islamic University of Malaysia, the *Pusat Islam* of UiTM University in Shah Alam, and the Universiti Putra Malaysia (UPM) in Serdang, in front of the then Vice-Chancellor and faculty deans of my alma mater the University of Malaya, and in front of audiences comprising university faculty members and students. Many were professors of eminence and repute.

I organized the launching of the book by the then Foreign Minister of Malaysia, now Tun Abdullah Ahmad Badawi. A lot of people attended – ambassadors, high commissioners, academics, consultants, trainers and friends. I was elated by my success in writing about the Prophet of Islam and publishing it. Some

10,000 copies of the English and Malay medium were sold it the first couple of years by Utusan Publications.

"The Messenger of God is an excellent model for those of you who put your hope in God and the Last Day and remember Him often."

[Qur'an, Al-Ahzab, The Allies, 33:21]

LOCATION-POINT MAP OF PROPHET MUHAMMAD'S ARABIA

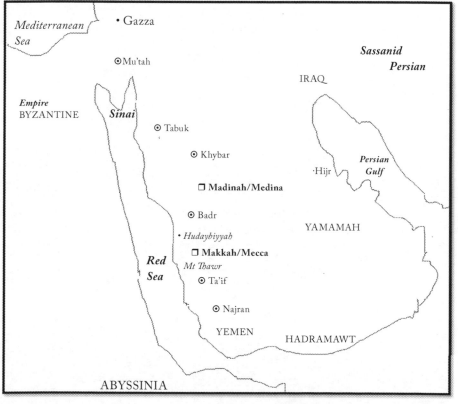

Source: Hand-drawn Map by Author

INTRODUCTION

Eulogies from the Outside

The author-analyst **Michael M. Hart**, in his well-researched book "The 100: A Ranking of the Most Influential Persons in History," credited Muhammad, the Prophet of Islam, who performed the triple role of a spiritual, temporal and political head, as being - in the annals of history - the foremost influential person on the face of the earth. The Prophet was highly efficacious not only as a religious and spiritual ruler, but also as a statesman, diplomat, military commander, administrator and community leader. In some of his book extracts are included commentaries from:

Alphonse de Lamartine, the celebrated French statesman and poet, who in the summation of his book, stated without any apologies whatsoever in his tribute to the greatness of the Prophet of Islam. He asked a pointed question that if greatness of purpose, smallness of means, and astounding results were the criteria of human genius, who could dare to compare any great man in modern history with Muhammad? As a philosopher, orator, apostle, legislator, warrior, conqueror of ideas, restorer of rational dogmas, of a cult without images, the founder of twenty terrestrial empires, and of one spiritual empire, Lamartine rounded up by asking that as regards all standards by which human greatness may be measured, was there any greater (leader) than Muhammad?

George Bernard Shaw, the celebrated English playwright, literary critic, and prolific writer, paid such a high tribute to the Prophet of Islam when he ascertained that he had carefully studied Islam and the life of its Prophet, stating that he had done so as a student of history and as a critic, and he had come to the conclusion that Muhammad was indeed a great man and a deliverer and benefactor of mankind. Shaw said that he had studied him – the wonderful man – and in his opinion, far from being an anti-Christ, the Prophet of Islam must be called the saviour of humanity. Such that he believed that if a man like Muhammad were to assume the dictatorship of the modern world he would succeed in solving the problems in a way that would bring the much-needed peace and happiness.

Annie Besant, the British social reformer and theosophist, underscored the contention that a Prophet of God must have divine authority for his claim, and that this must be evident to those who study his life objectively, even those not his followers. In her thesis, she observed that the essential sincerity of Muhammad's nature could not be questioned; and a historical criticism that blinked no facts, yielded nothing to credulity, weighed every testimony, had no partisan interest, and sought only the truth, must acknowledge his claim to belong to that order of prophets. She wrote that it was impossible for anyone who studied the life and character of the great Prophet of Arabia, who knew how he taught and how he lived, to feel anything but reverence for that mighty Prophet.

Perhaps one of the most favourable commentaries on Prophet Muhammad's greatness as a leader of distinction was the statement by a foremost European thinker, writer, historian and teacher, **Thomas Carlyle**, who in a series of lectures bearing the theme, "Heroes & Hero Worship," delivered a provocative talk entitled, "The Hero as Prophet," to a largely Christian audience on May 8, 1840. Among the eulogies Carlyle articulated on the Prophet of Islam (during a time when it was sacrilegious to praise the religion) included a description of the Prophet Muhammad as a man of truth and fidelity, true in what he did, in what he spoke and thought, noting that he always meant something; that he was a man rather taciturn in speech, silent when there was nothing to be said, but pertinent, wise, sincere when he did speak; always throwing light on the matter at hand; for that was the only sort of speech worth speaking.

Carlyle spoke at length about the Prophet of Islam, stating magnanimously, "*I mean to say all the good of him I justly can,*" and he elaborated in his delivery the defence of Muhammad against the false invectives and tirades of his enemies.

Jules Masserman, a Jewish American professor and psychoanalyst at the University of Chicago, laid down three objective standards for judging the greatness of leaders. He stated that leaders must fulfill three distinctive functions:

> 1. The leader must provide for the wellbeing of the led.
> 2. The leader must provide a social organization in which people feel relatively secure, and
> 3. The leader must provide his people with one set of beliefs/values.

In his analysis and assessment of history's great leaders, Masserman concluded:

> *"Perhaps the greatest leader of all times was Mohammed, who combined all three functions. To a lesser degree, Moses did the same."*

Professor K.S. Ramakrishna Rao, a renowned Hindu philosopher, in his book *"MUHAMMED – The Prophet of Islam,"* was said to have quoted the arch-criminal Adolf Hitler as saying:

> *"Leadership means the ability to move masses of men. The union of the theorist, organizer, and leader in one man is the rarest phenomenon on this earth; therein consists greatness."*

Professor Rao concluded, in his own words:

> *"In the person of the Prophet of Islam, the world has seen this rarest phenomenon on earth, walking in flesh and blood."*

Diwan Chand Sharma, another Hindu scholar, in his writing *The Prophets of the East*, also narrated:

> *"Muhammad was the soul of kindness, and his influence was felt and never forgotten by those around him."*

The Prophet was a leader of men, undisputedly so. Malaysia's fourth Prime Minister, Tun Dr Mahathir Mohamad, in his address to the Harvard Club in Kuala Lumpur, on January 18, 1996, cited the Prophet as being way up in stature among the great leaders of world history, followed in ranking by other acknowledged great leaders like the four Islamic caliphs, Jesus, Moses, Sulaiman the Magnificent, Mehmet II, Akbar the Great, Saladin Al-Ayyubi, Napoleon Bonaparte, Alexander the Great, Mother Teresa, and Nelson Mandela. In an authentic Tradition *(Hadith)*, the Prophet's cousin, **Ali ibn**

Abi Talib, was reported to have quoted the Prophet as having said, in answer to the former's question about the Prophet's basic character assets:

> *"Knowledge is my principal possession*
> *Reason, the root of my religion*
> *Love, my foundation*
> *Longing, my coach*
> *Remembrance of God Almighty, my weapon*
> *Patience, my dress*
> *Contentment, my prize*
> *Poverty, my glory*
> *Abstinence, my calling*
> *Obedience, my measure*
> *Striving (jihad), my character.*

Ibn Khaldun (1377), acknowledged as the foremost Arab historian who developed one of the earliest non-religious philosophies of history (his masterpiece contribution being the well-known thesis *Muqaddimah*), provides the modern world with a list of qualities of a genuine leader:

> *"Desire for goodness and good qualities such as generosity, forgiveness*
> *of error, tolerance towards the weak, hospitality towards guests, the*
> *support of dependents, patience in adverse circumstances, faithful*
> *fulfillment of obligations, liberality with money for the preservation of*
> *honour, respect for the religious law, and for the scholars who are*
> *learned in it…great respect for old men and teachers, acceptance of the*
> *truth in response to those who call for it, fairness to and care for those*
> *who are too weak to take care of themselves, attentiveness to the*
> *complaints of supplicants…avoidance of fraud, these are the qualities*
> *of leadership." (p. 285)*

All these qualities are cherished in the Islamic value system and were fully reflected in the *Seerah* or life history of the Prophet Muhammad.

The essence of this guidebook is to focus on the role of the Prophet as an exemplary leader who should be emulated by others: politicians, social entrepreneurs, managers, administrators, non-governmental leaders, counselors, military commanders, coaches, parents, teachers, public officials, community and spiritual leaders, and the like.

The term 'role' used here is significant in understanding the concept of leadership. Its original usage was in the theatre, when an actor takes part in a play, portraying a character or function. Thus when we use the phrase 'role model,' it denotes a person who is regarded by others as a significant example of a particular role, perhaps either as coach, counselor or mentor. It displays the hallmarks of leadership in striving to balance the traits of adulation and humility, with the vision to inspire others to attain greater heights of attainment.

For the modern managerial leader, this guidebook is a useful alternative supplement to the many existing references on the subject of leadership and management. The true benchmark on leadership, however, is found in the *Sunnah and Seerah* of the Prophet Muhammad, and they are applicably relevant for all times. The Prophet's qualities and attributes as an individual person and as a team leader are synonymous with the best requirements of exemplary leadership.

In the context of modern leadership criteria, it would be interesting and beneficial to cross-relate Prophet Muhammad's personal leadership style and its application with some of the modern concepts and principles studied in today's schools of leadership and management.

Leadership models propounded over the last half a century can be classified as modern, and the attendant attributes of the transformational-type leader will be an interesting analysis in this cross-comparison between the Prophet's leadership style of more than 1,400 years ago with today's style of leadership.

Questions like: was his leadership style 'situational' or categorised as a 'one-best style' would be briefly examined in our analysis. It would be tenable at the outset to say that although the Prophet was human, his coming was by divine inspiration. His attributes collectively fall into the term ***altruistic servant leadership***. This term will be defined in some detail in the introductory chapter of this book, which can suitably be regarded as a training manual for personal and organizational development. What is important to state is that Prophet

Muhammad's leadership among men was God-inspired, and his capabilities as a total leader have withstood the test of time and events.

The concepts enveloping the quintessence of Prophet Muhammad's leadership include coverage of the noble principles of:

- Justice and equity ('Adl bil-qist)
- Mutual consultation (Syura)
- Wisdom (Hikmah)
- Etiquette of dissent (Adab al-ikhtilaf)
- Felicity (Al-falah);

and these are embraced in tandem with:

- Perseverance, courage and discipline
- Perpetual gratefulness and enthusiasm
- Egalitarianism
- Integrity
- Righteousness
- Constancy of purpose, and
- Responsibility, authority and accountability

In this guidebook, an overview analysis is given on how the Prophet's life pervade into his multifarious roles as:

1. A Visionary Turned Transformational Leader
2. An Entrepreneur *Par Excellence*
3. A Manager-Administrator-Judge-Diplomat *Extraordinaire*
4. An Organizational Team Leader
5. A Strategist as a Military Commander
6. A Loving Family-Oriented Man
7. The Bearer of a Lifelong Legacy

Some of these roles will be adequately dealt with, and workshops comprising handouts/exercises/role-plays/simulations/mini case-studies/and test instruments that relate to modern precepts will be interspersed in this guidebook wherever relevant. It will help the trainer or facilitator engage in explaining and relating to the Prophet's wonderful attributes as a leader of distinction.

This guidebook embraces a stand-alone set of modules, nine in all. It is hereby cautioned that the presentation of the modules constituting the core contents of this guidebook needs to be done by a trained facilitator. It is to be noted that this guidebook is not meant to be an academic text for research purposes. Rather, it is to be used as a useful training and development guide for judicious facilitation at an interactive workshop session or at a discourse benchmarked on the Prophet Muhammad's leadership. While this guidebook is not intended to be an exhaustive analysis into all aspects of the Prophet of Islam's life as a unique multi-faceted leader, it will certainly help in fulfilling the objective of enabling the willing teacher or learner be a better future mentor or leader of people. It will certainly be useful to anyone who performs the role of a *da'i* or conveyor of the Prophet's eternal message to humankind.

<u>Questions to answer arising from this introductory section</u>

❖ Please summarise what the foreign scholars and analysts say about the Prophet Muhammad as a leader of influence.

❖ What relevant aspects can we transfer from the lessons of the early 7th Century leadership style of the Prophet Muhammad into the 21st Century?

❖ Why is there a need for the 21st Century leadership to be altruistic and egalitarian in its form and substance?

CHAPTER 1

The Leadership Function

The essence of Islam is that it is not only a form of worship or religion *per se*. It is all-pervasive in its embracement. It is what is known as the ***Ad-Din***, a complete way of life for the believers who totally subscribe to the **Oneness of Allah** and the dignity of Muhammad as His final and noblest Messenger. The sanctity of Islam pervades the realms and multifaceted dimensions of life on earth with the attendant rewards in the Hereafter (*Akhirah*).

The purpose of being a Muslim believer and leader is universal. The basic tenet is to enjoin good and forbid evil (*'amar ma'ruf nahi munkar*) – and by extension, to be a social master and an economic leader – just as Prophet Muhammad was during his time.

The Muslim leader is continually interacting with his community and environment. He or she is perpetually striving for excellence, in pursuit of the true meaning of right-doing (*Ihsan*) which consistently advocates continual acts of righteousness. In doing so, the leader is obliged to serve the interests and wellbeing of the community, the *ummah*, and not for self-interest or ingratiation. The principles of justice with equity, equality, mutual consultation, freedom of expression, and etiquette of dissent signify the virtuosity of the sanctity of the faith. The leader who abides by the love for Allah God Almighty, the Prophet and the believers will engender peace and goodwill throughout the community of nations.

It is important to note that in almost every chapter of the Qur'an, there is reference to right-doing as the lynchpin to faith. The most quintessential way of existence on earth, which is promised the bountiful reward in the Hereafter, is to diligently comply with the lifelong teachings of the holy Qur'an and the Traditions (*Sunnah*) of the exalted Prophet of Islam.

The Prophet's devoted wife A'ishah once described her husband Muhammad's character as the personification of the Qur'an, 'the translation of the Qur'an into practice'. By that she meant that he fully embraced and totally practised the teachings of the holy book, which contains the commandments of God Almighty, with all their stipulated intentions. The *Sunnah* exemplifies the legal way or ways, orders, acts of worship and statements of the Prophet that have become examples to be followed by all Muslim believers. The Traditions (*Hadith*) personify the Prophet's exemplary character, verbalisations, and conduct that serve as good examples to follow. Such a mentoring created the most substantial influence on the spiritual, moral, and ethical transformation of the *ummah* in both the major centres in and around Makkah and Madinah during and after the Prophet's time.

The Prophet's ultimate mission in life had always been the personification of the tenets of the Qur'an, without reservations. His commitment was, needless to say, one of total quality, based on implicit faith (*Iman*), fear of Allah the Almighty (*Taqwa*), and right-doing (*Ihsan*).

The concept of *Iman* is based on a strong belief in monotheism, the Oneness of Allah (*Tawhid*), and the sanctity of the Prophet as His final Messenger. The orientation to *Taqwa* is based on compliance with all the commandments of Allah the Almighty, and those who do so are the most righteous of believers. Righteousness, as exhorted in the Qur'an (5:2): *"Help you one another in righteousness and piety. But help you not one another in sin and transgression. And fear Allah. Indeed Allah is severe in penalty."* To commit wrongdoing would incur the wrath of the Creator, and instil fear in the wrongdoer.

Ihsan conveys the meaning of engaging oneself at the highest levels of deeds and worship, always striving for a level of perfection. The contention is that when you worship Allah or do good deeds, consider yourself as if you see Him and if you cannot achieve such a feeling or attitude, then you must always bear in mind that He definitely sees you.

Aside from being a spiritual leader, Prophet Muhammad was also *de facto* the head of state of Madinah in the earlier period of the 7th century. As head of state he was a splendid diplomat who earned the utmost respect of most foreign sovereigns and even political despots.

Islam exhorts its leaders to extol, first and foremost, the virtues of concern for human welfare. A leader must always lead by example. Hence the Prophet is the noblest exemplar. The welfare function of the Islamic state was particularly emphasised by the Prophet in the city state of Madinah when he affirmed, 'any ruler who is responsible for the affairs of the *ummah* but does not strive sincerely for their wellbeing will not enter paradise with them' (Riyadussalihin Hadith No:654). The Companions of the Prophet who eventually succeeded him clearly understood this welfare role as is evidenced by the emphatic statement of one early Caliph, Umar ibn al-Khattab: "The best of men in authority is one under whom people prosper and the worst of them is one under whom people encounter hardships."

When the Prophet founded the first Islamic state in Madinah based on *Syari'ah* or Qur'anic principles, he advocated the establishment of a welfare state that was egalitarian in its governance, focusing on full political, social and economic equality for all people. It was free from any wilful exploitation of the poor and the corruptible concentration of wealth in the hands of only a privileged few.

From the Islamic perspective, leadership is a trust (*amanah*) that involves the judicious use of authority, and with it comes responsibility (*taklif*) and accountability (*mas'uliyyah*).

With regard to the trilogy of responsibility, authority and accountability, Prophet Muhammad operated from the power-base of an all-inclusive supreme leader. In terms of responsibility, he was aware of his functions and roles as a leader to comply with and fulfil the obligations specified in the Holy Qur'an. Authority was entrusted by divine authorisation, which was duly acknowledged by his Companions. The leader needs to have the authority for the overall welfare of his people, team, or organization. Ibn Taimiyyah, a notable scholar, aptly commented,

"The exercise of authority for the people's benefit constitutes one of the greatest religious duties, without which neither religion nor a well-ordered world can be established."
- [Ibn Taimiyyah, *al-Siyasah al-Shariyyah fi al-Ra'I wa al-Ra'iyyah, 1955*]

The Prophet's realisation that he had to perform to the Supreme Creator's expectations was most demanding and he had to be accountable to make things happen for the overall benefit of the *ummah.*

Thus, no one was left out in receiving the attention and benefits of the state's programmes. The Prophet was mindful to remind all the appointed governors of the provinces that Islam held dearly to the principal codes of good governance: (1) the one who will be dearest to Allah on the Day of Resurrection will be the just ruler (*Imam*) and the one who will be most hateful to Allah on the Day of Resurrection, and will receive the severest punishment will be a tyrannical leader [Rawahul Tirmidhi]; and (2) he also cautioned the people's leaders that if anyone was put by Allah in positions of authority concerning the affairs of the *ummah* but chose to shy away from dealing with their followers' needs, plight, destitution and poverty, then Allah will not be bothered to deal with their own needs, plight, destitution and poverty when they themselves came to seek help [Sunen Abu Dawud].

The Muslim leader, whether *de jure* or *de facto*, must be guided by his understanding of the contents and the obeisance of the teachings of the Qur'an, and consequently the *Sunnah* or *Hadith* (Traditions) of the Prophet of Islam. Scholars are in consensus that embracing the *Shari'ah* of Allah involves a leader's commitment to:

1. Justice with equity (*'Adl bil-Qist*)
2. Rights and obligations (*Huquq*)
3. Mutual consultation (*Syura*)
4. Public interest (*Masalih*)
5. Success in this world and the Hereafter (*Al-Falah*)

The Muslim leader today faces severe challenges in the 21st century new era, just as Prophet Muhammad did in the 7th century *Jahiliyyah* era of ignorance. The *Ulil-amr*, a term used in the Qur'an to refer to 'those in charge of affairs,' (Qur'an 4:59), are collectively responsible to globally challenge the spread of corruption, terrorism, financial crises, and climatic degradation – which have been the consequences of bad leadership programmes and decisions. Being aware and embracing the Prophet's leadership model will be a positive beginning to transformational leadership.

One splendid definition of leadership that relates to the Prophet of Islam's model, *par example*, is as follows:

"If, by your very own thoughts, words and actions, you can inspire others to aspire to greater heights of achievement, then you are a leader."

— Dr Ron Liamsi

Questions to answer arising from Chapter 1:

1. How critical is leadership from the Islamic perspective?

2. Is *Ihsan* a core concept in Islamic leadership? Define and explain

3. How different is leadership in Islam from conventional leadership?

CHAPTER 2

Prophet Muhammad's Leadership Model (The Benchmark for Personal and Organizational Development)

What is Leadership?

The study of **leadership** is a fascinating and useful subject for mankind. Leadership, when it is effective, determines the wellbeing of families, organizations, nation states and the world at large. The leadership function is pervasive, encompassing all aspects of life on earth – be they social, political, economic, environmental, or legal.

Leadership is defined as "any action or process carried out by a leader that focuses on the utilisation of key resources towards the attainment of a beneficial outcome." Action is a dynamic word implying initiative, agility, and freedom of movement to do something good. A leader should act when faced with a problem or when arbitrating, and certainly when a critical decision needs to be taken. It requires the element of proactivity on the part of the leader to nudge and spur people to action when it matters.

In its essence, leadership is a process, not really a personality. Doing things right (efficiency) is just as important as doing the right things (effectiveness). The appropriate term that is used for being both efficient and effective is efficacy. The ultimate function of an efficacious leader is to lead followers towards a common or shared goal. Hence, arriving at the attainment of a shared goal is most likely to bring about a <u>beneficial end</u> to the outcome.

A leader always strives to achieve results with a positive outcome. In Islam, all acts to obtain results must be *Syari'ah*-compliant, and must be based on the desire to seek the pleasure and blessings of Allah the Almighty.

"Say: Verily my prayers, my acts of obedience, my life and my death are all for the sake of Allah, the Lord Sustainer of the worlds!"

[Qur'an, Al-An'aam, The Cattle, 6:162]

Leaders function to leave behind a legacy. While leaders seem to be abound, it would be pertinent to say that only the leaders who can make a difference towards enhancing the lives of people are the ones who are worth studying, emulating and remembering.

A leader may have all sorts of great ideas or vision, but if they are not put to action or implemented, then nothing gets done. The leader has become ineffective. While it is true that aforethought or strategic thinking is necessary before a leader can act, he should not ponder lengthily into a state of inaction. He should not become dysfunctional. A leader must have a certain degree of responsiveness to act judiciously, with relative speed if he is to seize the opportunity presented before him. In this, modern leadership precept is not radically different from what leaders in past history used to perceive. This comparative study is as relevant for us today as it was more than 1,400 years ago during the time of the Prophet of Islam.

A leader also needs to be <u>focused</u>. He leads not only by directing, as the word focus implies, but also *par example* or *bil-hikmah*, with measured steps and wisdom. Hence the call for *Leadership by Example*.

Professor John E. Adair, of the Industrial Society (U.K.), who is known to have carried out extensive research on the subject of leadership, wittily stressed that, *"a gram of example is worth a kilogram of exhortation,"* which suggests that a leader should also practise what he preaches. In a similar vein, a true leader asserts his substantiveness by conveying that his word is always his bond.

As stated earlier, leadership is not all about directing. Followers (*jama'ah*), or team members united with a mission (*harakah*), especially in the modern context, do not like to be bossed around. They prefer to be treated as equals, for they each consider themselves to be valuable contributors in the quest for excellence when pursuing the <u>attainment of a common objective</u>.

The term '**stewardship**' is appropriately used in this context to refer to the role of the vicegerent (*khalifah*) as the representative of God Almighty on earth. *Khalifah* means 'representation'. Man is given the trust by the Creator to prosper the earth he lives on, and thus by extension the trust being given is for the greater good of society. The office of vicegerency denotes Allah's blessing to man's rightful place to inherit the earth, with specific faculties, abilities and competencies to help prosper the earth he lives on. Even when the angels questioned God Almighty on the creation of man as a *khalifah*, He cautioned them:

"And (remember) when your Lord said to the angels: 'Verily, I am going to place (man) generations after generations on earth.' They said: 'Will You place therein those who will make mischief and shed blood, – while we glorify You with praises and thanks and sanctify You?' He (Allah) said: 'I know that which you do not know."
[Qur'an, Al-Baqarah, The Cow 2:30]

Altruistic leadership, servant leadership, or stewardship – each appellation is interchangeable – is a reference to anyone who assumes the task of, first and foremost, sincerely serving the needs of others more than for one's own self. To regard ourselves as stewards, to put the needs of others first – these are some of the critical elements of creating a fresh approach to leadership that is in consonance with the one demonstrated by the Prophet of Islam. Such a leadership is not a prerogative of position, authority or power. It is referent-based. It operates on the natural capacity to work closely with others, not just through others, interdependently.

In the holy Qur'an, this attribute is termed *harisun*, which means having utmost concern for the welfare of others. It starts with the natural desire to serve first, then making a conscious choice to lead. The leader is distinctly different from the person who wants to lead first because, more often than not, of a desire for power or to acquire material wealth.

Sayyid Mawdudi, another renowned scholar, once commented:

"The rights and powers of the caliphate of God, and in this respect all individuals, are equal…no one can deprive anyone of his rights and powers. The agency for running the affairs of the state will be established in accordance with the will of individuals…"

We have the whole phalanx of prophets, saints and a list of egalitarian leaders such as Caliph Umar Al-Khattab, Saladin Al-Ayubi, Mahatma Gandhi, Martin Luther King, Nelson Mandela, Ramon Magsaysay, Tun Abdul Razak and Mother Teresa and others to testify to this.

Stewardship is the substance that emphasises the use of openness, persuasion and influence – rather than exclusiveness, control and manipulation. Stewardship is putting service to others ahead of self-interest. The test of altruistic, servant leadership is when we choose service over self-interest most essentially to build the capacity of the ensuing generations to empower and govern themselves. It is an inside-out pathway to leader-follower synergy; creating an emotional partnership with those we share power in tandem with the desire to get results with, rather than, through people.

In terms of modern organizational development (OD) planning, it has to do with redesigning and re-engineering structures and practices, rethinking the role of bureaucratic functions, changing financial practices to close the budget deficit gap, reorienting or adjusting the human resources systems and practices – for the overall good.

Altruistic service leadership is a practical philosophy, which is ascribed to people who choose to serve the well-being of others first, and then lead, as a way of extending service to the people and the nation. There is a *hadith*, which reported the Prophet as having said, "The leader of a people is (veritably) their servant." The root word of service is serve, which in this context means to give homage and obedience to. In the Islamic connotation, it means to be perpetually subservient to the will of Allah the Almighty.

The Muslim leader will internalise by first asking himself, "Who am I?" The answer has to be, "I am the servant and in the service of Allah," as a vicegerent (*khalifah*) on earth. This stance is based on two specific verses in the Qur'an:

"Behold, thy Lord said to the angels: 'I will create a vicegerent on earth.' They said: 'Wilt Thou place therein one who will make mischief therein and shed blood? – Whilst we do celebrate Thy praises and glorify Thy holy (name)?' He said: 'I know what ye know not."

[Qur'an, Al-Baqarah, The Cow 2:30]

"It is He Who sends down manifest Ayat (proofs, evidences, verses, lessons, signs, revelations, etc.) to His slave that he may bring you out from darkness into light. And verily, Allah is to you full of kindness, Most Merciful."

[Qur'an, Al-Hadid, The Iron, 57:9]

Being subservient to Allah, God Almighty, is to comply with all His commandments (*Taqwa*) as stated in the Qu'ran. It implies the orientation towards good-doing on earth that is liked and blessed by Him.

"Say: 'Verily, my prayer, my sacrifice, my living, and my dying are for Allah, the Lord of the 'Alamin (mankind, jinn, and all that exist)."

[Qur'an, Al-An'aam, The Cattle 6:162]

Humility and dedication to service underscore Islam's benchmark quality on leadership. When Islam was dominant under the leadership of the second caliph, Umar al-Khattab, he aptly surmised that "there is no pomp and ceremony in Islam." Thus when in later medieval Islamic period, during which leadership was peppered with despotism and basic neglect of Prophetic guidelines, the sanctity of the faith's discipline was affected by such willfulness of the leaders of the time.

The leadership paradigm that is recommended for use as a benchmark for efficacious personal and organizational development is evidenced in the Prophet's Altruistic Service Leadership (ASL) model. To structure and develop an organization towards a desired level of excellence, a pragmatic and enduring framework has to evolve. The model used must provide a standard or benchmark for hands-on practitioners in the areas of leadership and management.

Thus managerial and like-minded leaders are encouraged to adhere to what is now popularly referred to as the "Three plus Four plus Five Leadership Model" (3 + 4 + 5 Model) of the Prophet of Islam.

Let us first begin by taking note of what God Almighty says:

"Allah has promised such of you as believe and do good works, that He will surely endow them with (the institution of) khilafah on the earth."

The Prophet Muhammad himself pointed out and reminded that everyone who is a believer is entrusted by God Almighty to be a *khalifah* or a shepherd.

"Every one of you is a shepherd and everyone is responsible for what he is shepherd of."
[Sahih Bukhari and Muslim]

Leadership in Islam is central to the Islamic personality and this has been greatly exemplified by Prophet Muhammad who had himself exhorted the *da'iyah* (a person engaged in *da'wah* or the spreading of the message of good-doing) to assume the role of a leader, either *de jure* or *de facto*, as one who enjoins others to the straight path – to *ihdinas sirat al-mustaqim*.

The Prophet Muhammad showed that a good leader encourages his followers to serve others to get ahead in life. As a leader, one is bound by a position of divine trust to be responsible and accountable for executing justice, equity and consensus in all affairs of life. A leader could be a father, a community head, an administrator, a manager, a social worker, a supervisor or even an influential worker. Much of his spirituality can be found in his advocacy of filial piety, loyalty to family, and strong affiliation to the noble teachings of the Qur'an.

Muslims, especially those aspiring to be leaders of distinction, are asked to model themselves after the Prophet Muhammad and his Companions and the enlightened thinkers and leaders who patterned their life individually after him.

"Verily in the Messenger of Allah you have an excellent example for him who looked unto Allah and the Last Day, and remember Allah much."
[Qur'an, Al-Ahzab, The Allies 33:21]

A well-known Prophet's tradition (*hadith*) states:

"Every one of you is a custodian and is responsible for what is in his custody…the ruler is responsible for what is in his custody and so is every man and woman."

The Prophet himself had cautioned:

"Be not weak in character nor simply do what others do, whether good or bad. Rather make up your minds: you may follow others in good deeds but not when they do something wrong."

The role of the leaders who are in charge of the affairs of the community is pervasively critical – as in the case of the judge in court, member of parliament, state secretary, government minister or head of state – each serving with public authority – must also be the protector and custodian of the public interest. The public service leader, sometimes referred to as the civil servant, must always be open to sincere advice (*nasihah*) as well as constructive criticism (*mu'aradah*).

The efficacious leader must also be a dynamic listener. When somebody took exception and forthrightedly criticised the second Caliph Umar al-Khattab, one of his senior lieutenants moved assertively forward to deal with the complainant's rudeness. To which the caliph interjected, "No, let him speak. No good will come of us if we do not listen."

The Muslim leader, in the footsteps of the Prophet Muhammad, is exhorted to strive to create the highest standards attainable in every sphere of work that his organization is engaged in. Serious efforts should be made to negate vices and corruption.

The core vices that are destructive to good leadership are lying, breaking a promise, and betraying people's trust. The Prophet's *hadith* says:

"There are three things, which, if a man practices secretly, he is a hypocrite, even though he fasts and performs the worship: if, when he relates something, he lies; if, when he makes a promise, he breaks it; and if, when he is given a trust, he betrays it."
[Rawahu Bukhari and Muslim]

Thus in some ASEAN Muslim countries like Indonesia, Malaysia and Brunei the teachings of the 12th century Islamic theologian, Imam Al-Ghazali, hold sway advocating moderation, integrity and humility for the development of good character in man. This implies that we have to be moderate, simple and respectful in asking for our wants and needs. We should avoid excesses and extremities in life. In advocating a state of equilibrium in one's pursuits, Al-Ghazali gives the analogy of the ring of fire.

The ring of fire represents our desires in life. We are caught in it. The best place to be in this ring of fire would be at the centre, as it would be the coolest spot within it! A similar metaphor is in the idiomatic expression, 'in the eye of the storm.' When a hurricane hits and you are in its path, and everything gets blown asunder, the best place to seek cover for safety is in its epicentre – in the eye of the storm. Let's now analyse in the following pages the Altruistic Service Leadership framework.

Altruistic Service Leadership

The Merriam-Webster Dictionary defines it as "unselfish regard for or devotion to the welfare of others." The English Oxford Dictionary defines Altruism as "regard for others as a principle of action."

The Qur'an states, *"Verily, there has come to you a Messenger (Muhammad) from amongst yourselves (i.e. whom you know well). It grieves him that you should receive any injury or difficulty. He (Muhammad) is anxious over your welfare (to be rightly guided, to repent to Allah, and beg Him to pardon and forgive your sins in order that you may enter Paradise and be saved from the punishment of the Hereafter); for the believers (he is) full of pity, kind and merciful."*
[Qur'an: At-Tawbah, The Repentance, 9:128].

In this verse, the altruistic character *(harisun)* of the Prophet of Islam is evident. The word *altruistic* is derived from the Latin word *alter* (plural *alteri*) which means 'others,' and in the context of our analysis it implies a sincere concern for the welfare and wellbeing of others; and while 'others' connote the *ummah* and fellow human beings they also include the animal kingdom, the environment, the flora and fauna, and the future generations to come.

Altruistic Service Leadership

The aim of the Altruistic Service Leadership model is to bring about a changed mindset, a paradigm shift from self-centredness to sincere concern for the wellbeing of others. It is based on the tenets of the Qur'an and the Prophet's Sunnah, but it is vital to underscore at the outset that the principles espoused are universal and applicable to all *sans* considerations of ethnic origin, race, creed, religion or culture.

What is important is to serve the commandments of God Almighty and meet the varied rising expectations of the community (the *ummah*). As leaders, we are expected to serve the interests of the community at large. Whether we are operating as civil servants in the public sector, or as suppliers and vendors in the private sector, we serve to fulfil the rising expectations of our clients or customers. The tagline for the aspiring leader is, in short, Serve to Lead!

What is important is to serve the commandments of God Almighty and meet the criteria of good self-governance. The journey can begin with the realisation that a leader must develop the hallmarks of a change master:

The hallmarks of a change master, game changer or transformational leader are when he can positively address the following critical issues:

- Faith in God Almighty
  "There is no God but Allah, and Muhammad is His Messenger"
- Vision of Greatness -
  "What legacy do I want to leave behind?"
- A Sense of Mission -
  "I pass through this world but once. Any good therefore that I can do for my fellow beings, let me do it now. Let me not defer it, for I shall never pass this world again!"
- Agility –
  "How can I ensure that I am able to move physically quickly and easily and able to think quickly and clearly?"
- Passion and Compassion –
  "How can I develop a powerful feeling for enjoining good and forbidding evil, and cultivate a strong feeling of sympathy and sadness

for the sufferings and bad fortunes of others, but most importantly to be able to do something to help out?"

- Humility with Self-Esteem –
  "How do I develop the quality of not being proud but humble because I am continually aware of my own shortcomings that could be improved upon? Equally important, I should refrain from consciously making myself noticeable and attention-grabbing by being modest in my quest for excellence."
- Willingness to Learn –
  "I should cultivate the habit of continuous lifelong learning and the wisdom to seek the truth."
- Abiding by the Golden Rule: Treat Others as You Would like to be Treated –
  In the realm of interfaith relationships, I should always remember to treat others as I would like to be treated.
- Be Decisive, after resorting to God's Guidance –
  In key matters, I should pray for God Almighty's guidance and having done so make a decision in full faith of a positive outcome.
- Being the Best
  I must aspire to attain the best results in whatever I do!

The 3 + 4 + 5 Altruistic Service Leadership Model

(The 3 Dimensions, 4 Postures and 5 Tenets)

The Leadership Framework

• <u>**The Three Dimensions**</u>

The character profile of the Altruistic Service Leader begins with the three (**3**) *Dimensions* of life, the four (**4**) *Postures*, and the five (**5**) *Tenets*.

Let us first look at the three dimensions first: ***Alignment, Empowerment,*** **and** ***Attunement***, which if collectively and sequentially embraced will bring about the positive desired outcome called ***Felicity*** through ***Synergy***.

The framework for managerial leadership action begins with the first dimension: **Alignment**, which refers to commitment to *Tawhid*, the Unity of God Almighty, with God-consciousness as the essence. *Tawhid* is the most basic principle of Islam, as it also envelops the role of man as the vicegerent and custodian of Allah on earth, ruling in conformity with Allah's will. It envelops the Vision of Greatness to help create a world order that is peaceful, sustainable and prosperous. This needs to be done in tandem with a Sense of Mission, for it is senseless to pursue an overriding goal in life without total commitment (*iltizam*) with the element of accountability, and a constancy of purpose (*istiqamah*). Leadership emerges from God-consciousness, a vision of the outcome of good-doing, knowledge, insight and virtue, commitment, with courage and humility. These are the ingredients of wisdom (*hikmah*).

The second dimension is **Empowerment.** Man is empowered by God Almighty to be a *khalifah*, the vicegerent, to help prosper the world he lives on. It is a trust given to him to realise his pivotal role in organizational development. The *khalifah* is entrusted by God Almighty to be responsible for managing and administering worldly affairs, abiding by the Prophet's obligatory qualities of honesty (*sadiq*), trustworthiness (*amanah*), advocacy (*tabligh*), and wisdom (*fatanah*).

Konosuke Matsushita, the founder of the Matsushita industrial empire, named this category of person the *ningendo* man. *Ningendo*, or the 'Way of Man' is the path man must follow based on the awareness that he is endowed with the ability to be the master of all things on earth. Matsushita was said to be not formally schooled, but he made tremendous efforts to study the goodness of all the major faiths, in particular Buddhism, Christianity and Islam. Thus when he set up his academy, the PHP Institute (PHP = Peace, Happiness & Prosperity) to train the *ningendo* managerial leaders of his vast industrial empire, he had superimposed the concept of *khalifah* and *al-Falah* to build the human resource capabilities of his huge teams of people.

The third dimension is **Attunement.** This orientation is reflected in the daily acts of faith that are collectively known as *Ibadah*, interspersed with shared values in action. It is the observance of enjoining good and forbidding evil (*amar ma'ruf nahi munkar*). It is the continual acts of good-doing (*ihsan*) that render ourselves subservient to God Almighty. It is the burden of proof to demonstrate that as leaders we do not just pay lip service to what we have pledged to do for the benefit of others. Attunement is the sum total of the acts of faith (*ibadah*), the passion and compassion to do well and prevent wrongdoings. It incorporates shared values in action, such as mutual respect, courtesy, courage, humility, and support.

When all these dimensions have been embraced in real practical life, then we have a situation where **Felicity** (*Al-Falah*) via synergy prevails. This state of affairs provides the synergy, the attainment of happiness, success and prosperity for all who share the common vision of greatness. Within this enveloping framework, the leader has to be mindful of the methodology and personal value systems that substantiate and contribute to the realisation of the overriding vision of a managerial or community leader in the role of a vicegerent.

The 3 Dimensions

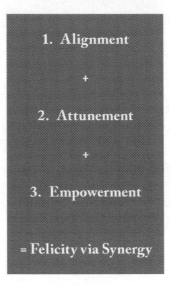

1. Alignment

+

2. Attunement

+

3. Empowerment

= Felicity via Synergy

- ### <u>The Four Postures</u>

Within this framework, we move on to the next phase of the Prophet's leadership model: the **Four (4) Postures**. The term 'postures' here refers to the effectual behaviour characteristics the leader (*amir*) needs to possess and sincerely exhibit. The first of these is **justice, with equity** (*'adl bil-qist*). This is followed by **mutual consultation** (*syura*), **freedom of expression** (*hurriyah al-kalam*), and the **etiquette of dissent** (*adab al-ikhtilaf*).

Justice with equity (*'Adl bil-qist*) is the core thrust of Islamic organizational leadership. Justice (*'Adalah*) is derived from one of the beautiful Names of God. It is a condition in which things and beings are placed in their rightful and proper places. Justice, which is based on the *Syari'ah*, requires the leader to be absolute and just, fair and square, evenhanded and impartial and righteous in his dealings with people and situations.

Justice and fairness are expected of Muslim leaders in all their dealings, even with their enemies. Allah commands:

"O you who believe! Be steadfast witnesses for Allah in equity, and let not the hatred of any people seduce you into dealing unjustly. Deal justly, that is next to piety. Observe your duty to Allah. Lo! Allah is informed of all that you do."

[Qur'an, Al-Ma'idah, The Food, 5:8]

The concept of equity (*istihsan*) is concerned with considerations of fairness and conscience, especially in cases which do not find a fair solution under the rules of positive law. This is because the rules of law are usually formulated in an objective manner and style, and do not consider the peculiarities of specific cases and situations. The law may thus be applied to a case but the result may be less than satisfactory and fair. It is in such predicaments that Islamic law's *istihsan*, and equity in western jurisprudence, can play a useful role. In specific circumstances, he has to employ the principle of natural justice to ensure that feelings are not hurt and relationships are not disrupted. This is to assure that the absoluteness or sternness of certain codes would not appear to be unfair if practised or implemented to the letter.

In a leader, justice must be seen to be done. Prophet Muhammad adjudicated all cases referred to him by God Almighty's supreme laws:

"Give (thy) judgment in accordance with what Allah has revealed. Be not influenced by their wishes; and beware of them lest they make thee depart from some injunction given thee by Allah."

[Qur'an, Al-Ma'idah, The Food, 5:49]

The Muslim leader has to deal with all kinds of people, but especially his followings, with a sense of justice and fairness, regardless of race, creed, nationality or beliefs. The Qur'an commands all Muslims to be just and equitable, even when it involves those opposed to them.

"O you who believe! Stand out firmly for justice, as witnesses to Allah, even as against yourselves, or your parents or your kin, be he rich or poor, for Allah can protect both. So follow not the lusts (of your hearts), lest you may avoid justice, and if you distort your witness or refuse to give it, verily, Allah is ever well-acquainted with what you do."

[Qur'an, An-Nisaa', Women, 4:135]

Al-Mawardi (d.1058), the author of a well-known treatise on governance, highlights several qualities of a good leader, which he summarises into three:

- ☐ Just character (*Adalah*)
- ☐ Knowledge (*Ilm*), and
- ☐ Wisdom (*Hikmah*)

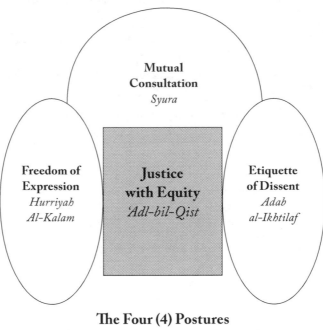

The Four (4) Postures
(Justice with Equity as the core)

In cases where empathy is called for, it is the mark of a leader to exercise patience and temperance, without excesses. Such restraint, for the benefit of the overall good, displays the attributes of humility and compassion on the part of the leader.

"It is part of the mercy of Allah that you do deal gently with them. Were you severe or harsh-hearted, they would have broken away from about you. So pass over (their faults), and ask for [Allah's] forgiveness for them, and consult them in affairs (of the moment). Then, when you have taken a decision, put your trust in Allah. For Allah loves those who put their trust (in Him)."

[Qur'an, Al-'Imran, The Family of Imran, 3:159]

Perhaps the most comprehensive verse in the Qur'an that stresses the importance of justice is when Allah the Almighty says:

"Verily, Allah enjoins Al-'Adl (i.e. justice and worshipping none but Allah Alone – Islamic Monotheism) and Al-Ihsan [i.e. to be patient in performing your duties to Allah, totally for Allah's sake and in accordance with the Prophet's Sunnah (legal ways) in a perfect manner], and giving (help) to kith and kin (i.e. all that Allah has ordered you to give them, e.g. wealth, visiting, looking after them, and any other kind of help), and forbids Al-Fahsha (i.e. all evil deeds like illegal sexual acts, disobedience of parents, polytheism, telling lies, giving false witness, taking a life without right), and Al-Munkar (i.e. all that is prohibited by Islamic law: polytheism of every kind, disbelief and every kind of evil deeds), and Al-Baghy (all kinds of oppression). He admonishes you, that you may take heed."

[Qur'an, An-Nahl, The Bee, 16:90]

These should be the overriding considerations for everything that we say or do in life, individually or collectively. In all aspects we should strive for *jihad*, continuously striving to search and pursue the truth. We recite the Qur'an many times over, but we must also try to understand its meaning and message. We talk of the *Sunnah* of the Prophet, but oftentimes this is more related to appearances. We must pay more attention to the Prophet's character attributes of love, kindness, honesty, fairness, truthfulness, sincerity, fulfilling promises, and so on.

Mutual consultation (*Syura*) is the interactive group communication process that must be adhered to by those in positions of authority and responsibility in order to encourage a sense of participation and collective commitment to the attainment of a worthwhile cause or goal. When problem-solving and decision-making are called for, a consensus-seeking mechanism is employed. The objective is to arrive at a solution that is pragmatic and acceptable to all involved in the undertaking. The decision arrived at should be by consensus, but based also on majority decision (*al-kathratu-hujjatun*) should there not be total agreement. The leader appointed to lead the *syura* process should be the most knowledgeable and experienced on the subject matter at hand.

The process of *syura* is akin to the Japanese *nemawashi* (consensus-seeking) or Western 'brainstorming' session. The Prophet Muhammad engaged in the process of mutual consultation based on the exhortation in the Qur'an, and it is important to note that Allah the Almighty has made the process obligatory. He even aligned it with the all-important obligatory worship of prayers (*solat*), payment of tithes (*zakat*), and good-doing:

"*And those who answer the Call of their Lord [i.e. to believe that He is the Only Lord (Allah), and to worship none but Him Alone], and perform As–Solat (Iqamat-as-Solat), and who (conduct) their affairs by mutual consultation, and who spend of what we have bestowed on them.*"

[Qur'an, Ash-Shura, The Counsel 42:38]

The Muslim leader is thus expected to continually engage in mutual consultation, based on the above-stated Qur'anic guideline. Consultative leadership entails engagement, interaction management, communication, collaboration and partnership, which also implies that leaders should continually strive to be connected, interactive, and maintain good relations with their followership.

Freedom of Expression (*ḥurriyah al-kalam*) is the right given to an individual to voice his concern, agreement or suggestion over any issue or matter which affects his or the community's welfare. The Prophet was adept at handling problematic issues brought before him. During *halaqah* or discussion sessions, the Prophet listened to the views of others intently, by the simple bodily act of leaning forward without interrupting, before commenting, advising, and coming to a decision.

While certain matters that need resolution find their direct solutions in the Qur'an, those that are not so apparent in the Holy Book are arrived at by referring to the Prophet's *Sunnah* or *Hadith*, or through the process of mutual consultation (*syura*), assertive reasoning (*ijtihad*), or consensus-seeking (*ijmak*). In strategically important matters like determining the fate of the Quraish in the Hudaibiyyah peace agreement, or when arriving at a decision whether to fortify Madinah or go on the offensive in the Battle of Uhud; or when making a decision whether the Quraish must pay a third of their agricultural produce to the state coffers, the Prophet engaged and arrived at such decisions by any or a combination of the aforesaid processes. He would actively partake in two-way communication through dynamic listening skills, being taciturn, and speaking only when necessary – sometimes even at the expense of his own views.

In the run-up to the Battle of Uhud, the Prophet noted that some of his followers were actively of the view that he should lead the offensive and fight the Quraish from outside Madinah, whilst others had advocated that the fight should be confined to within the fortifications of the city. While the Prophet himself preferred to stay within; but taking into account the more impacting general view of his followings (*jama'ah*), which expressed concern about the possibility of women, children, and the elderly being put at risk by the invading marauders, chose to do battle outside the city's walls instead.

It is evident that the Prophet of Islam encouraged his Companions to give their opinions frankly whenever he consulted them, even when their views differed from his own. He consulted them on matters over which there were no revelations, if only to accustom them to thinking seriously about problems related to the wellbeing of the community and the nation-state (the *ummah*). He underscored that consultation was useless if there was no freedom of speech in expressing oneself. The Prophet never blamed anyone for making a mistake when making his final decision. He emphasised that a leader is obliged to consult others, especially in matters concerning the welfare of the followers. The Prophet led the way in applying the Qur'anic injunctions when executing the principles of consultation (*syura*).

"… *and consult them in affairs (of the moment). Then, when thou hast taken a decision, put thy trust in God.*"

[Qur'an, Al-'Imran, The Family of Imran, 3:159]

In the above example, the Companions (*Sahabah*) took cognisance of the fact that although they had the right to express their opinions, they did not have the right to impose them upon the leader. It was sufficient for them to make their opinions clear, but they then had to give the leader the freedom to choose whichever of the opinions was the best. At Uhud, prior to the battle, when they realised that they had pressured the Prophet to go out of Madinah to defend the city-state and wanted to apologise, the Prophet retorted back, "Once a Prophet has donned battle dress, he should not take it off again until he has fought."

Thus, the Prophet Muhammad had taught them another important point in effective leadership: a leader should not waver once he has taken a decision and begun to act upon it, because doing so might shake the followers' confidence in him and create further confusion and doubt about his ability and competence.

Encouraging positive change for the better, especially change in the direction of social and moral improvements, makes it duty-bound for Muslim leaders to subject their social environment to continuous critique for the common good. The Prophet of Islam was quoted to have said, "Only two (kinds of men) may rightly be envied: a man whom God Almighty has given wealth and thereupon endowed him with the strength to give it away in the cause of justice; and a man whom God has given wisdom to and who acts in its spirit and imparts it (to others)."

The right to the freedom of expression of one's opinions in speech and writing is one of the fundamental characteristics of an Islamic state. This implies that the intellectual leaders of a community are morally bound to bring forth whatever new ideas they may have relating to the progress of the community, and to advocate such ideas in public. It must, however, be understood that such a freedom of opinion and of its expression (which today includes freedom of the press or the Internet via social media) must not be used for incitement against the law or sedition against the established government, and must not be allowed to offend against common decency.

The Prophet Muhammad himself has been described by a Western analyst, Thomas Carlyle, as taciturn in speech, speaking only when necessary; but that when he speaks the delivery is full of words of wisdom.

The main purpose of such freedom of expression must surely be to help enjoin any right-doing and forbid wrongdoing. One of the Prophet's traditions stated: "A community in the midst of which sins are being committed which could be, but are not, corrected by it, is most likely to be encompassed in its entirety by God's punishment." It is, therefore, in the interests of the whole community that its members strive for continued improvements of its social and moral obligations. God Almighty has proclaimed: *"Behold, Allah does not change a people's condition unless they bring about a change in their inner selves."* [Qur'an, Ar-Ra'd, 13:11]. While it is true that everything in life is fashioned by God Almighty, He indeed provides the opportunity for us to redeem ourselves to create a better life through our own sincere efforts.

Etiquette of Dissent (*adab al-ikhtilaf*) or the ethics of disagreement calls for proper decorum when argumentation and debate crop up during the processes of communication, consultation or dialogue. It is the mode by which the positive aspects of disagreement are encouraged. Muslim leaders must relearn the art and etiquette of agreeing to disagree, in the process discovering how the early generation of Muslim leaders put it to good use. Freedom of speech should not be shrouded by personal attacks on each other's character or viewpoints to create discord and hard feelings. Mutual respect based on 'feeling good about others' (*husnul-zhon*) must prevail at all times. Islamic interpersonal relations is based on good, not bad, intentions (*innamal-'amalu-bin-niat*).

A companion demonstrated how, under the guidance of the Prophet, one could object and at the same time maintain the highest levels of sincere courtesy and politeness. The episode related that prior to the Battle of Badr, Prophet Muhammad told his commanders and the outnumbered Muslim army (313 Muslims *vs* some 1,000 Quraish disbelievers) to camp at a certain location. The Prophet reckoned that it was a strategic spot to control the water supply and deprive the enemy of it in a desert battle. Hubab ibn Al-Jamuh of the Bani Salama clan who was a member of an advanced reconnaissance team, and knew well the area surveyed, saw that there was a more strategic place that if the Muslim army camped at, it would give them an upper hand in the outcome of the battle's fortunes.

Hubab was so devoted to the leadership of the Prophet that he did not merely say, "Well, if the Prophet said so, then why should I say otherwise?" He was proactive, not passive, and he was not rude. How then did Hubab give his opinion that may seem at odds with the prevailing opinion of the Messenger of God?

Here's how: Hubab courageously, but with all good intentions, asked of the Prophet, "O Messenger of God, is your opinion based on a revelation from God, or is it based on war tactics and strategy?" To which the Prophet replied, "No, it's based on war tactics and strategy." So Hubab proposed, "then this is not the most strategic place to pick because there is an alternative well-site that is closer to the enemy, halt there and close the wells behind it. He advised the Prophet to leave the wells of Badr behind him so that the Quraish army would not be able to use them for obtaining water. For the Muslim army, they should construct a cistern so they would have access to plenty of water supply. So the enemy would be deprived of water, feel thirsty and be unable to fight on. The Prophet accepted Hubab's tactical suggestion – a proposal that was one of the main factors that led to the victory of the Muslim force in this critical first battle against the forces of the disbelievers.

On another occasion, just prior to the Battle of Khandaq when Abu-Sufyan's 10,000 confederate armed forces posed a severe threat of attack on the Muslim city-state, it was told that a companion by the name of Salman al-Farsi had suggested the digging of a long trench around the more attack-prone side of Madinah.

While other companions of the *syura* council were prepared to meet the enemy in a frontal attack and defend the city from within, the Prophet saw the innovative side of Salman's suggestion, and accepted it. While some sources question the contribution of Salman, the truth was more probable that the Prophet himself had already thought about such a defence, but acceded to Salman's idea to encourage the process of *syura* to take effect. So the 9,000-yard trench was dug. The outcome was the retreat of the attacking Quraish-led confederate forces after they found the Muslim defences impenetrable and the prevailing weather conditions unendurable.

The justification for Allah to test the patience and perseverance of His true servants is through the etiquette of dissent. Dissentions and disagreements have become parts and parcels of human existence, yet the challenge of life's endeavours is for leaders to be able to seek consensual common ground with decorum and mutual respect, rather than in an aggressive, spiteful manner.

"And if your Lord had so willed, He could surely have made mankind one Ummah [nation or community (following one religion, i.e. Islam)], but they will not cease to disagree. Except him on whom your Lord has bestowed His Mercy (the follower of truth – Islamic monotheism) and for that did He create them."
[Qur'an, Hud, 11:118-119]

And further, whenever dissentions occur, the Prophet Muhammad advised us to be patient:

"A believer who mixes with people and is patient towards those who adopt hurtful attitude will gain greater reward compared to another who does not mix around with others and is not patient towards those who are hurtful in attitude."
[Rawahu Ibn Majah]

"Verily Allah likes those with courtesy/softness in (the execution of) all affairs."
[Rawahu Muslim]

In modern times, the Japanese people have practised a similar mode of decorum and etiquette of dissent. The renowned industrialist Konosuke Matsushita, in his book, *Thoughts on Man* (1982), recounted how the Japanese use the philosophy of *shuchi* to tap on the collective wisdom, or the wisdom of the many. This is akin to the Muslim concept of *syura*. Matsushita writes in his book:

"Shuchi, the wisdom of the many (collective wisdom), can forestall confrontations…it is the accumulated wisdom of everyone…not just of the great religious prophets like Jesus and Mohammed, but of every single person. When the separate wisdoms of the many are collected and – their differences reconciled – they become a greater single wisdom."

Matsushita further elaborates that a leader needs to exhibit possession of a *sunao* mind. This is akin to the Muslim *adab al-ikhtilaf* mindset, the mind that adheres to the etiquette of dissent. *Sunao* in Japanese means tractability, describing a person who is flexible, listens carefully to what others have to say, enabling him to see things as they actually are without adhering only to his own way of thinking. The *sunao* mind conveys love and respect, even those you hate. It helps to correct mistakes and perceptions that lead you to move in the proper direction.

Thus, *shuchi* cannot be produced by those who lack the *sunao* mind. Those who see only their own interests and respond only to their own emotions must necessarily come into conflict with others. But if a person has a *sunao* mind and handles issues and concerns through the *shuchi* approach, he does not become selfish and can therefore – in the family, group, organization, nation, or world – deal with other dissenting opinions fairly, learn from them, and attain a higher and happier level of existence. The *sunao* mind teaches the individual, especially the leader, that his mission lies in contributing to the mission of all humanity, and that he can work towards this goal even while his actions are at the same time not in perfect concordance with his own nature and desires.

• THE FIVE (5) TENETS

The four applied behavioural postures work in tandem with the **Five (5) Tenets**, amplifying the critical aspects of the Islamic value systems, namely:

(1) **personal integrity** (*al-kamal asy-syakhshi*), (2) e**nhancement of personal relationships** (*taqwiyyah al-shilah*), (3) **leadership efficacy** (*fa'iliyyah al-qiyadiyyah*), (4) **ethical conduct** (*makarim al-akhlaq*), and (5) **moral uplift** through spiritual knowledge (*tahzib al-akhlaq*).

Personal integrity, the first tenet in the context of this analysis, means "my word is my bond." It is the hallmark individual quality projecting the spiritual side of leadership. It is a values-based principle pegged on to character and beliefs rather than on technique and technology. The leader of integrity in the Islamic mould is classified as the servant-leader, with him being the servant (*'abd*) only of God Almighty. Acting as His *vicegerent* on earth, his accountability is uniquely pervasive and holistic. This is not quite unlike the servant-leader type purported by author-consultant Robert Greenleaf who, using the same term ascribed the great leader as a champion principally devoted to serving his people. The Muslim servant-leader devotes his priority first, to his relationship with his Creator, and then secondly to his relationships with his fellow beings – in that order (*Hablum-min-Allah, wa hablum-minannaas*).

Personal integrity is basically reflected in the leader's ability to keep covenants and trusts. Islam emphasises this. The covenant is with God Almighty, the *ummah*, and every other being he interacts with in the pluralistic community of nations. The sum total of keeping one's covenant, promise or pledge is very important since it shows one's central character. Thus when a leader gives his word to do something beneficial, he should feel accountable for its due performance. He is well aware of the interdependent link in the trilogy: responsibility-authority-accountability. In normal business parlance, personal integrity gives meaning to the idiomatic expression, "My word is my bond!"

> *"And fulfil the promise. Surely (every) promise shall be questioned about."*
> [Qur'an, Al-Isra', The Journey by Night, 17:34]

> *"O you who believe! Why say you that which you do not (do)?"*
> [Qur'an, As-Saff, The Ranks, 61:2]

Keeping trust implies that it is a big sin to commit a breach of it. A'ishah narrated (in *Sahih Bukhari, Vol.3. Hadith No.686)* that the Prophet Muhammad had bought some foodstuff on credit for a limited period and mortgaged his armour for it; and when the time came for settlement, he promptly redeemed the loan amount, true to his promise.

Keeping covenants and trusts is the forerunner to creating a legacy of greatness. In the Prophet of Islam's *Seerah*, an occasion to be remembered in the annals of Islamic history was the signing of the 628AD Treaty of Hudaibiyyah on the 6th year of Hijrah. A hadith narrated by Anas reported that the Quraish disbelievers made a treaty with the Messenger of Allah, imposing such terms that surprised even the Prophet's Companions. The terms of the treaty made out by the Quraish laid out as follows:

"Whosoever among you shall come to us, we shall not return him to you, and whosoever from us shall come to you, you shall return him to us. They (the Companions) said: O Messenger of Allah, shall we write this? 'Yes' said he, 'whosoever of us shall go to them, Allah will keep him away, and whosoever among them will come to us, Allah will soon find out a relief and a way for him."

Just as soon as the treaty was signed, a believer (*mu'min*) named Abu Jandal came to the Prophet in a state of perplexity and bewilderment, but the Messenger of Allah – true to the terms of the agreement – sent him back to Makkah.

In another episode, the Quraish clan had sent an emissary to the Prophet, and upon seeing the wonderful leader of Islam in person, the said emissary wanted to join the ranks of the believers and stay. True to the spirit of the covenant, the Prophet rejected the overture.

A companion by the name of Abu Rafe' reported the case of a Quraish clansman messenger who called on the Prophet Muhammad. As soon as he saw the Messenger of Allah, he was awed by the personality of the Muslim leader:

"The Quraish sent me to the Messenger of Allah. As soon as I saw the Prophet s.a.w., Islam was cast in my heart." Then I said, "O Messenger of Allah, I shall never return to them." Whereupon the Prophet said, "I do neither break a treaty, nor do I make emissaries prisoners. Therefore, return. If there remains in you what is now in you, come back." Then I returned. "Afterwards I came to the Prophet and accepted Islam."
[Abu Dawud, Vol.2.Chapter XXIII, pp.397-8, H:134]

The Companions were discomforted by the perceived give-away stance taken by their revered leader, but the Prophet Muhammad insisted that victory was theirs. This was evident when Allah the Almighty sent down a Qur'anic revelation which states:

"Verily we have granted thee a manifest victory!"
[Qur'an, Al-Fath, The Victory, 48:18]

This incident later underscored the farsightedness, courage and steadfastness of the Prophet in meeting his obligations as a leader of his expanding community of believers. When the Prophet and his followers finally entered Makkah in triumph after the treaty was abrogated (following a breach of the 10-year peace truce when a Quraish clan attacked an allied Muslim clan), the conquest was made easier with the bastion of support already established from within the holy city, where supporters like Abu Jandal and other believers had built and mounted sufficient resources within Makkah. They were thus able to welcome their long-departed brothers home again in triumph.

Personal integrity (*Ihsan*) is one of the critical character traits looked for among modern management practitioners. Professor Peter F Drucker, once the doyen of management gurus in the modern era, attested that integrity is crucial in human capital development. Integrity is basically the quality of being sincerely honest and having strong moral principles that cannot be short-changed. Integrity of character is the hallmark of the Prophet of Islam's wholesome persona and that of his best companion Abu Bakr as-Siddiq.

Working shoulder-to-shoulder with his fellow Companions in building the trench when preparing for the Battle of Khandaq, negotiating the terms of the Treaty of Hudaibiyyah with the opposing Quraish tribes and adhering to them, and dispatching his trusted lieutenants to various regional outposts with its attendant risks displayed the characteristic qualities of the altruistic prophet.

Allah has decreed,

"And if you are on a journey and cannot find a scribe, then let there be a pledge taken (mortgaging); then if one of you entrusts the other, let the one who is entrusted

discharge his trust (faithfully), and let him be afraid of Allah, his Lord. And conceal
not the evidence for he who hides it, surely his heart is sinful."

[Qur'an, Al-Baqarah, The Cow, 2:283]

In developing people, future leaders and successors, Prophet Muhammad focused on the tacit value of personal integrity. It was narrated by Abdullah ibn Abbas: Abu Sufyan told me that Heraclius said to him:

"When I inquired of you what he (Prophet Muhammad) ordered you, you replied
that he ordered you to establish prayer, to speak the truth, to be chaste, to keep the
promise and to pay back trust." Then Heraclius added, "These are really the qualities
of a Prophet."

Integrity holds considerable inner power at its source. It hinges on the capability of the leader to guide, direct and influence his people based principally on moral principles and ethical values related to standards of good behaviour, fairness and honesty. Such a quality, supplemented by righteousness, trustworthiness and foresight, moulds people and ideals together.

Enhancement of Relationships, the second of the five tenets, is critical for building understanding, rapport and respect for each other. According to Peter Sheldrake, an early 21st century human capital development consultant who delved into the realm of servant leadership, leaders should have the capacity to treat everyone as a human being and not just as a unit of production, as in a factory.

Sheldrake echoes servant-leadership guru Robert Greenleaf's contention that people must undertake a journey in life together, and undertake that journey with mutual respect. People are no longer units of production, but are working together, thinking together, and moving forward together. Values-driven issues are important in the continuous and planned efforts to developing better relationships: such as the growth of people, their caring, healing, and community-building. The critical human elements of passion and compassion must prevail.

One of the United States of America's extremely successful industrialists, Andrew Carnegie, once said:

"You must capture and keep the heart of the original and supremely able man before his brain can do its best."

It was reported that when the Prophet of Islam dispatched Muadz bin Jabal, the brilliant military strategist, to Yemen as the province's governor, the Prophet called out to him thrice as he was riding away to his destination, *"O Muadz, make sure you govern with justice!"* In this context, the administration of justice would begin by leading from the heart. If one had the opportunity to lead others, the goodness of the heart should always come first, and that good things would follow. The secular way of leading is usually direct from the head (IQ) and relies strongly on critical thinking.

To lead from the heart, a leader needs to:

- courageously lead from the front
- show sincere appreciation of the genuine contribution of others for the cause
- sell the vision, by exciting team goals, and
- build relationships of trust and support

As a Prophet, but also as a human being, the Prophet Muhammad had to ensure that time was the essence in all his undertakings as a leader of substance, and as the paragon of excellence. He was the forerunner to the modern concept of multi-tasking by prioritising. He scheduled his activities according to their priorities, as exhorted in the Qur'anic chapter *'As-Asr,* (The Time) 103:1-3,

1. By *Al-'Asr* (The Time)
2. Verily, man is in a state of loss
3. Except those who believe *(in Islamic Monotheism)*
4. And do righteous good deeds
5. And recommend one another to the truth
6. And recommend one another to patience

The Prophet's list of priorities included: the continued conveyance of Allah's message far and wide; advocacy of the religion of Allah among the ranks of disbelievers; striving to counter the constant threats posed by the disbelievers and thus protect the sanctity of Islam; initiating and implementing multiple peace treaties; overseeing the laying down of arms; implementing *hudud* laws in crime prevention; conducting military campaigns to ensure eventual peace and security; sending out functionaries to collect tithes to be used for the development of the state and the welfare of the *ummah*; and specifically laying down rules and regulations for the just administration of a new Islamic state.

The Prophet Muhammad was reported to divide his time of day into three proportions: one principal proportion for Allah, one proportion for his family, and one proportion for himself. The latter he divided between himself and the *ummah*. While the remembrance of Allah was always in his heart and mind, he scheduled time judiciously for the other two proportions, which were in all cases for the cause of Allah.

The time he allocated for his people was best given to the commoner more than to the elite. The Prophet also praised the leader who showed empathy with his people, who reached out to their needs. He showed his displeasure against the kind of leader who distanced himself from the masses. The Prophet did not give to himself without considering the needs and interests of others first. He was inclined to show preference for the people of merit and would devote greater attention to those who excelled in pursuit of the *Din*. He was constantly concerned about the welfare of his people. Until his last dying breath, the Prophet was reportedly heard uttering in whispered tones, "my people, my people, my people…" (*ummati, ummati, ummati…*)."

Truly, the Prophet's model offers a universal and holistic worldview of relationships among people, and this is best adduced from a divine commandment to humankind at large:

"O mankind! We have created you from a male and a female, and made you into nations and tribes, that you may know one another. Indeed the most noble of you in the sight of Allah is the most righteous of you."

[Qur'an, Al-Hujurat, The Chambers, 49:13]

From this verse, mankind is asked to interact and enhance relationships on a global basis, regardless of political, ethnic, cultural, or spiritual affiliations. This is evidently becoming necessary today in the world of cross-border trade and internationalization. It is important, when interacting with the various nations and communities constituting the *ummah*, to keep abreast with decorum and

courtesy, regardless of social status or creed. A'ishah, Prophet Muhammad's
beloved wife, related that she heard the Prophet praying to God Almighty:

*"O Allah! When a person who is placed in authority over my ummah (people) is
oppressive on them, be Thou strict with him, and when such a person is kind on them,
be Thou also kind on him."*

[Hadith Muslim, from Al-Nawawi's *Riyad al-Salihin*]

And the Qur'an is also emphatic on this, that kindness and politeness in a leader's
dealings with people should pervade in all situations where communication is
essential:

*"And speak to mankind with courtesy and politeness (according to the best standards
of human speech)."*

[Qur'an, Al-Baqarah, The Cow, 2:83]

A'ishah reported how the Messenger of Allah had responded, when he was
accosted by some Jews:
"May death come upon you (As sam'alaykum)." To which A'ishah retorted, *"And
upon you, and may Allah curse you and the wrath of Allah descend upon you."* Upon
which the Prophet interjected,

"Gently, O A'ishah, be kind, and keep yourself away from roughness."

[Rawahu Bukhari]

To begin with, the building of interpersonal relations can be as simple as
daily verbalising and practising the age-old basic **Golden Rules of Human
Relations**:

> ☐ The SIX Most Important Words
> **"I'm Sorry I Made a Mistake"**
> ☐ The FIVE Most Important Words:
> **"You Did a Good Job"**
> ☐ The FOUR Most Important Words:
> **"What is Your Opinion?"**
> ☐ The THREE Most Important Words:
> **"If You Please…**
> ☐ The TWO Most Important Words:
> **"Thank You!"**
> ☐ The ONE Most Important Word:
> **"We!"** (Not "I").

In the search for fulfilment, Prophet Muhammad was always looking for feedback. He was narrated as having said:

"Those who are present should convey things to those who are absent and you should let me know about what is needed by people who cannot convey their needs to me. On the Day of Rising, Allah will make firm the feet of a person who conveys to a ruler the need of someone who cannot convey it himself."

With feedback, Prophet Muhammad managed to receive first-hand information about his performance, from which he was continually able to evaluate whether his mission was on target. In doing so, he had to keep constant contact with all his Companions, field commanders, aides and in Madinah – with all the Ansar communities who were the true supporters and believers of his cause. With an excellent information system on stream, he was able to plan and strategise his options for the immediate and long term pursuit of his goals.

Leadership efficacy, the third tenet, is perhaps the most significant personal leadership test for the altruistic servant leader. The overriding question that a leader should ask is, "When I leave this organization (or indeed this world), what legacy do I leave behind?" The Malays in Malaysia have a well-known quote that asks, *"When the tiger dies, it leaves behind its stripes; but when a man dies, what does he leave behind?"* This is a strategic question that needs to be asked by everyone who is born in this world destined to serve the community at large.

Efficacy means not just doing things right, but more importantly doing the right things in work and life. It is being both effective and efficient in the same breadth. When inspiring others to change from a life of darkness to light, as the Prophet of Islam did, it is not sufficient for a leader to merely deliver a series of rousing speeches. Compelling words of encouragement and wisdom are essential to uplift the followers' spirit, yet one can be taciturn without verbalising mere rhetoric. The Prophet was well aware that deeds and actions moved his followers, not merely words. Great leaders know that their examples are emulated. But leading hands-on through humility is how true leaders make vision, aspirations and shared values tangible. They provide objective evidence of personal commitment to the cause. They live by the ethos: *"The legacy you leave behind is determined by the life you choose to lead."*

Every leader, nay every person, is a vicegerent of God Almighty on earth. He or she will want to ask the vital question, "When I leave this world, what legacy do I leave behind for my fellow beings?"

When Prophet Muhammad made his last pilgrimage to Makkah, he stood on Mount Arafah before a large congregation of followers, finally looked up and asked, *"O Allah, have I completed my mission?"* For the ordinary human being holding the mantle of leadership, the question could be rephrased, "Have I done my job, as a vicegerent (*khalifah*) on earth?" It is the ultimate strategic question for the leader at any level.

When the Prophet of Islam humbly posed this question, Allah, God Almighty, responded by sending down the last verse of the Qur'an:

"This day, I have perfected your religion for you, completed My favour upon you, and have chosen for you Islam as your religion."
[Qur'an, Al-Ma'idah, The Food, 5:3]

This verse bears testimony to the fact that the Prophet Muhammad had completed his mission and left the legacy of the religion of Islam, the religion of peace, for humanity. To this day, with some 1.5 billion Muslim followers in the world, Prophet Muhammad is the altruistic servant leader the world was waiting for, as in the words of the noble Qur'an:

"Surely, a messenger has come unto you from among yourselves; grievous to him is that you should fall into trouble; he is ardently desirous of your welfare; and to the believers he is compassionate, merciful."

[Qur'an, At-Tawbah, Repentance, 9:128]

Ethical Conduct, the fourth tenet, is all about right-doing. This tenet or principle that a leader should hold on to determines the net worth of a leader in the spiritual sense. Ethics originates from the Greek word *ethos,* which means character or custom. In modern parlance, ethos refers to the distinctive disposition, character and attitude of a specific people, group or culture (e.g. the Malaysian ethos echoed by the clarion call *"Malaysia Boleh!"* or *Malaysia Can!* and now *"1Malaysia!"*). Ethics covers individual character, including what it means to be a good person within the confines of the social rules that govern good behavior, in particular the legal and social rules regarding what is good and evil (for the promotion of good governance).

Shari'ah is the law of Allah Almighty. It lays the foundation for the Islamic *Din* or way of life. In the secular legal systems, the law and ethics are not necessarily interrelated. People may adhere to the laws but they need not necessarily be ethical in their outlook and behaviour. Sheldon Amos, in his book, *The Science of Law* says: "A man may be a bad husband, a bad father, or a bad guardian without coming into conflict with the rules of a single law." Shari'ah is the law that is based on ethics; its basic values being universal and permanent. It deals with the inward and outward. The rules of Shari'ah cannot be fulfilled without sincerity, true intention, love, mercy, compassion and respect for the law itself and the Law-Giver, Allah the Almighty.

The purpose of Shari'ah is to develop good persons within an upright, civil society. It is impossible to have a society compliant with Shari'ah and yet have injustice, ugliness, cruelty and evil within it. Any rule that departs from justice to oppression, from mercy to viciousness, from giving benefit to causing harm, and from wisdom to futility, is not from the *Shari'ah* of Allah.

In the modern organizational setting, ethics also refers to the adherence to a code of professional conduct. The motivation behind positive ethics is to do good all the time while striving to do better the next time – like the continuous improvement technique the Japanese industry refers to as *kaizen*. The Muslim advocates what is known as *iltizam* (the will to make good workable) and *istiqamah* (with constancy of purpose).

Moral Uplift through Spiritual Knowledge, the fifth tenet, refers to spiritual knowledge (as opposed to mere secular knowledge) as a basis for spiritual uprightness and religious inspiration, to do good to humankind and to all others. Spiritual orientations based on values-driven religious teachings have rendered some of the world's top chief executives of organizations a high spiritual quotient (SQ), to perform better on the job.

It protects the systematic and comprehensive way of life (*Din*), fosters the life (*nafs*), preserves the progeny or family (*nasl*), develops the intellect (*'aql*), and protects property or wealth (*mal*). The purpose of Islamic Law (*Syari'ah*) is to promote ethics and morality in our daily life.

The fundamental principles of morality show how Islam shapes human action. Moral norms in Islam have been translated into twelve main values, with the Unity of God being the first. The other eleven are:

1. Honour your parents.
2. Render unto others what is due to them.
3. Deal kindly with the orphans.
4. Calibrate the measure when measuring and weigh with the right balance.
5. Fulfil your promise.
6. Slay not your children fearing becoming a victim to poverty.
7. Slay not the life which Allah has forbidden, save with right.
8. Come not near unto adultery.
9. Follow not that where of you have no knowledge.
10. Walk not in the earth exultant.
11. Squander not your wealth in wantonness but take the middle path.

When leaders strive to establish a hygienic, ethical and moralistic society, we will see the establishment and development of:

- a clean and health-conscious society because Muslim believers and followers abide by the principles of purification (*taharah*), purificatory bathing (*ghusl*), and ablution *(wudu')*;

- a systematic organizational movement *(tanzim haraki)* because we have learned the lessons of praying in a congregation (*jama'ah*);
- a system of social entrepreneurship because we have learned the purpose of giving alms and tithes (*zakah*); and a
- a unified universal community that transcends borders because we have learned the values gained from the pilgrimage when peoples from all over the globe meet (*Hajj*).

A leader must, first of all, be a good follower, adhering to the *syari'ah* (the Islamic law based on *Al-Qur'an* and *As-Sunnah*), and is ethically and morally bound by the Islamic code of behaviour and conduct when dealing with others, whether they are Muslims or non-Muslims. Thus the only leader to be obeyed is he who follows God Almighty's precepts and the teachings of the Prophet.

The core premise of Islamic-oriented leadership is that man is the servant of the Creator; hence he functions as a servant-leader. True leaders have one abiding quality – the moral will to persevere. Moral power rests upon qualitative values like a sense of purpose, pride (with humility), patience, perseverance and perspective (prioritisation).

When the holistic 3 + 4 + 5 Altruistic Service Leadership formula is properly understood and embraced, it will bring about **Felicity** (*Al-Falah*), through Synergy and Success.

The Five (5) Tenets	1. Personal Integrity (My Word is My Bond!)
	2. Enhancement of Relationships (What plans and actions can I institute to continually improve relationships?)
	3. Leadership Efficacy (When I am gone, what legacy do I leave behind?)
	4. Ethical Conduct (Good-doing: enjoining good and forbidding evil)
	5. Moral Uplift through Spiritual Knowledge (My strength is derived from the Qur'an and my Prophet's example)

A leader or would-be leader must bear in mind that whilst he seeks success and happiness, he is certainly not free from the trials and tribulations of life. The Prophet once said:

"Be mindful of Allah, you will find Him before you. Get to know Allah in prosperity and He will know you in adversity. Know that what has passed you by was not going to befall you and that what has befallen you was not going to pass you by. And know that victory comes with patience, relief and affliction, and ease with hardship."
[Rawahu Tirmidhi]

A leader can fail or be derailed in seeking success and happiness for several reasons, some of the major ones include:

Inner causes

- [ ] Not remembering Allah, God Almighty
- [ ] Succumbing to one's lusts (greed, sex, and hedonistic orientations)
- [ ] Sheer arrogance (pride before a fall)
- [ ] Harbouring bad thoughts about others (because of envy, jealousy, and having inferiority complex)
- [ ] Not using the God-given power of reason before acting
- [ ] Lacking ethical-moral fibre, thus displaying mental-behavioural dissonance

External causes

- [ ] Keeping bad company
- [ ] Listening to poor advice
- [ ] Tendency to please others who are more influential, status-wise
- [ ] Overwhelmed by external, secular, physical developments, thus becoming spiritually dehydrated

The modern leader who seeks to embrace the transformational Altruistic Service Leadership model (by putting into practice the 3+4+5 = Felicity through Synergy formula) will be able to substantially help sustain growth and advancement, and will be contributing, at least in the short-term, to the 21st century generation's sustainable development needs. A worthy target for the modern leader to attain will be the United Nations' Millennium Development Goals (MDGs) set for the year 2015 onwards. The MDGs is a set of eight international development goals that were agreed upon by all 189 United Nations member states at the time, with at least another 23 international organizations to help achieve the following goals by year 2015:

1. Eradicate extreme poverty and hunger
2. Achieve universal primary education
3. Promote gender equality
4. Reduce child mortality
5. Improve maternal health

6. Combat HIV/AIDS, malaria, and other diseases
7. Ensure environmental sustainability
8. Develop a global partnership for development.

Questions to answer arising from Chapter 2:

1. What is the role of leadership in human life activity?

2. Why is Altruistic Service Leadership (ASL) critical in today's extremely capitalistic environment?

3. How can a leader fail due to inner and external causes? Specify some of them.

4. Describe your understanding of the 3+4+5 = Felicity through Synergy model. Test its application to the attainment of the United Nations'-sponsored Millennium Development Goals (MDGs).

CHAPTER 3

A Visionary turned Transformational Leader

Vision of Greatness

The world, nations, states, organizations, institutions, and even families need visionary leaders. While vision is an essential element of transformational leadership, such leaders are rare. Prophet Muhammad was one of the earlier visionary leaders of distinction. He had a vision of greatness.

It is said that if the measure of leadership is only the exercise of unquestioned authority, then anyone who happens to occupy a position of power can be called a leader. By this definition, then all sovereigns, presidents, prime ministers, chief executives, judges, police chiefs, and school principals can be classified as leaders because they significantly use positional authority. And of course, many parents too use authority (often combined with a good measure of punishment and coercion) to get their children to obey them. Yet the ability to only command-and-control does not make one a visionary leader, let alone a genuine transformational leader.

The Visionary Leader

Nations need visionary leaders, and vision is the critical element of transformational leadership. To start with, why are there so few visionary leaders? The answer is that very few adults have any vision at all. Even those who think they have one seem to be ambiguous about what their vision is all about. Remember the age-old classic tale in the Middle East and India of the 'Six Blind Men and the Elephant'? And what did Helen Keller, the blind inspirational educator, say about having a vision? She said that many people have the ability to see but have no vision, whilst she did not yet she had a clear vision of what life should meaningfully be.

So who is a visionary leader? A visionary leader perceives challenges and growth opportunities before they occur, making the environment ready for their people to produce extraordinary results and outcomes that make real, meaningful contributions to life and the world at large. So names like Robert Kuok of Malaysia, Prof Muhammad Yunus of Bangladesh, Prem Rawat of India, Bill Gates of America, and Nelson Mandela of Africa, crop up as leaders with visions of greatness for the future.

According to futuristic strategic consultant, Howard Silverfarb, "a visionary leader has a clear mental picture of a desirable future that gets his hands off the rear-view mirror and place them onto the steering wheel…putting him in touch with the inductive approach, to get where he wants to go. The vision needs to be compelling. It essentially takes the cue from the Greek proverb,

"You must know to which port you are going before you leave harbour."

So the first challenge is to get those in positions of relative power to think about the future, rather than have them regress into the past. The strange thing is that if you ask a four or five year-old child what he/she wants to be in the future, they are excitedly clear about what they want to become: a nurse, teacher, fireman, policeman, soccer player, or an actor. However, when they become teenagers, they seem to have lost such a focus, and give vague answers about what they want to become. They have become lost in a world of hedonistic orientations. Those sparing few young people who do try and talk about the future will parrot back what their parents expect them to be: become a professional and make lots of money! Thus many a parent would gleefully say with pride, "My son, the lawyer…" or "My daughter, the doctor…"

The general lack of visionary leadership worldwide arises from a number of individual and social factors. Some of the more significant ones are as follows:

☐ Regressing into the past

People at work spend very little meaningful time thinking and planning about their future. They tend to reflect mostly about what happened in the recent past. They prefer to dwell upon and relive the events of the day, the little stupid actions of the little Napoleons at the workplace, and the small egotistical slights of the rich, famous and powerful. Try asking, "What do you think the economy will be like in six months?" And they will most probably evade the question and talk mostly about what hit them in the past. They do not spend enough time thinking about the future, and sadly many young professionals are simply incapable of thinking out into the future.

☐ Imagination, creativity, and innovation lacking

As a would-be leader, have you ever experienced your teacher, parent or boss asking you to close your eyes and imagine the future? If you ask a number of college or university students, they will most likely respond, "never". In fact, if you were a college student or even an employee, caught with your eyes closed, you would be labeled a slacker whiling away the time doing nothing beneficial. Blame it on the education system that focuses mainly on the usage of the left brain: on language, analytical, logic-based thinking process. We need more right-brain thinkers to produce visionary leaders. At the very best, we need creative whole-brain thinkers to become the thought-leaders of the century.

☐ Lack of parent-teacher support

Modern-day parents and some teachers often discourage the evolution and usage of imagination. By nature, children tend to live in a world of fantasy anyway; so it would be relatively easy to induce them to dream possibilities… to become visionary. Yet many parents assume that for their children, vision equals fantasy. This assumption is more destructive than constructive. It is critically important for leaders to develop vision, and it is even more important for leadership to be visionary.

Transformation Management
(The Process of Managing Change)

Transformation infers profound, exponential change. Islam brought about a dramatic change in the individual and collective life of the inhabitants of Madinah because of its inclusive insight and comprehensive outreach into all aspects of the life in the city state.

When Islam spread to Madinah, the Prophet Muhammad established the concept of nation-state and bound all previously warring and contentious tribes and factions to it. The new Islamic state was founded upon a constitutional and spiritual base, and from there it expanded to unite the whole Arabian Peninsula, for the first time in Arabian history. This was a landmark development in the political history of the Arabian Peninsula.

The *Hijrah* (Emigration) became the watershed in the establishment of a Vision of Greatness for the spread of Islamic civilisation. The events which ensued bore testimony to the soundness of the farsighted Prophet's teachings and training of his dedicated band of followers. They collectively showed themselves capable of shouldering the responsibility and fulfilling the accountability of being Allah's vicegerents on earth to execute the divine laws meant for mankind, to fulfil His commandments, and to always strive for excellence in His path.

At the time of emigrating, the Prophet Muhammad was already 53 years old, and his close companion Abu Bak'r was 51, but absolutely nothing could hinder their resolve to attain their mission of establishing a just Islamic state in Madinah, for the cause of Allah the Almighty.

The message of Islam is to organise the obligation to worship (*ibadah*) based on the monotheistic upholding of the principle of the Oneness of Allah and to foster inter-human relationships in the context of universal acceptance and tolerance for each other in daily social and business activities (*muamalat*). This makes up the rationale for life's existence. In order for it to be realised, it requires a dedicated following in the form of a disciplined *ummah* community and a territorial base.

In Islam, the order of life is regulated by the commandments, stances and bearings brought to light in the holy Qur'an and exemplified by the Prophet's

Sunnah (examples, instructions and interpretations of it). The laws and guidelines contributed to the moulding of the nation-state in which the most ideal society that has ever emerged in human history developed. It is the model by which Muslims everywhere and at every moment must abide by to ensure for themselves the true meaning of success in this world and the Hereafter.

Muslims are exhorted and warned to stay away from self-inflicted misery arising from the triple negative influences of *syaitan* (satan), *syubahah* (bad company), and *syahwat* (lustful desire). The dire warning is that there is no hope of salvation except by total submission to Allah the Almighty and following the traditions of His beloved messenger.

The Transformational Leader

To begin with, transformational leaders are not transactional in character. They are very few in number and are prime movers and shakers, possessing personal charisma. They have very lofty goals and superior ideals. They are also seen as people of high integrity. Transactional leaders, on the other hand, focus more on a series of 'transactions,' being interested much more on looking out for themselves, with an orientation towards a give-and-take attitude that is based on an exchange of rewards and punishments to reach pre-determined goals.

Transformational leadership is oriented towards developing an attractive and challenging vision, together with the followers. The leaders then tie the vision to a strategy for its achievement through progressive action steps towards full implementation. Transformational leaders create greater commitment through shared values in action, with themselves being in the thick of action. Transformational leadership conveys a style that is described as leadership that creates a valuable and positive change in the followers. A transformational leader focuses on 'transforming' others to help each other, to look out for each other, to be encouraging and harmonious, and to look out for the organization in a holistic way. It is in this style of leadership that we see the leader as a highly motivational, inspirational and continually in a performance-driven mode. Such is the style predominant in the Prophet Muhammad.

Transformational leaders are assertive risk-takers who seize opportunities when they arise. They are also systems thinkers who understand and value people interactions, culture and technology. They seek to create a continuing climate of excellence by setting the highest standards in every sphere of work that the organization is engaged in – systems, structure, and people, by benchmarking against the best. In the case of the Prophet of Islam, the benchmarks were already established in the divine commandments and guidelines provided in detail in the holy Qur'an, where evidences, proofs, verses, lessons, signs, revelations, etc., are amply explained in the form of *Ayats*.

Change Agent *Extraordinaire*

The true leader who is an agent of change *par excellence* is exemplified by the sacrifice, self-denial and multi-faceted qualities of the Prophet Muhammad. Even by the modern world's discerning standards, perhaps even more so today, the Prophet's character and personality become worthy of emulation. The role and contribution of one single man to spread the universal message for all mankind was phenomenal enough to warrant special mention in the annals of history. And yet he was not a make-believe gargantuan leader.

The Prophet of Islam was essentially a simple man of peace and integrity. He was genuine, and saw himself as an ordinary human would see himself. When he had time available from the affairs of state, he would busy himself with household chores; he would patch his own clothes, sweep the floor of his house, do the family shopping for necessities, and mend his own shoes. During the construction of the Prophet's mosque in Madinah, he would toil as hard as any other worker on the job, sometimes even more.

Indeed, to those not familiar with the daily happenings in the city-state of Madinah, it was truly difficult to differentiate the doings of the Prophet from those of the commoner on the street. The Prophet Muhammad was reported to have said:

"Man has no claim to other things other than a house to live in, a cloth to cover himself with, bread to sustain himself, and water to quench his thirst."

The Prophet of Islam was a change agent *extraordinaire* who transformed the Arabian political, social and spiritual landscape beyond anyone's expectations. In a land rife with the practices of idolatry, fornication, crime, corruption, greed, gambling, alcoholism, child-killing, wife-beating, fratricide, factionalism, moral excessiveness, and general societal disorder, it became a monumental task for any leader to set about the task of initiating reformed exponential change. But with courage and the will (*iltizam*) to persevere in the face of adversities, Prophet Muhammad began the continuous overwhelming task (*istiqamah*) of redesigning and reengineering the framework of life within the Makkan, and later, the Madinan, communities.

Mounting a massive campaign to spread the message and facing the challenge of empires, the Prophet called on his fellow Companions and vicegerents to show profound and impacting leadership, but not with total impunity. His influence was such that even when he was unavailable at the scene they would emulate his way of doing things to get the job done.

In modern management leadership in the search for excellence, celebrated researchers such as Tom Peters and Nancy Austin attested that the current best-style set of attributes would encompass leadership as a sacrifice, self-denial, love, fearlessness, and humility. It is in the perfectly disciplined will. This, they said, is also the distinction between great and little people. The harder you work, the harder it is to surrender. The role of the leader is to enhance, transform, coach, care, trust and cheerlead. The activities of the leader are to educate, sponsor, coach, and counsel, using appropriate timing, tone, consequences, and skills. Well said. Such were also the attributes of the Prophet of Islam.

The transformational leader embraces what researchers Bass & Avolio (1993) in the modern context call '**the full range of leadership**' model. It embraces four elements:

1. **Individualised consideration**: which focuses on the degree to which the leader attends to his followers' needs, acting as a coach, counselor and mentor. This leader shows empathy and support, keeps communication open and places challenges before the followers. There is mutual respect, celebrating when success is achieved; and followers have the will and aspiration for self-development. Such was the relationship between the Prophet Muhammad and his companions like Abu Bakr and Muadz bin Jabal.
2. **Intellectual stimulation**: the leader challenges assumptions, takes calculated risks, and openly solicits followers' ideas. Learning is a critical value factor, where followers are invited to be creative, pose

questions, think deeply about issues at hand, and continually find better ways to execute their tasks. Prophet Muhammad's relationships with Ali ibn Abi Talib and Salman al-Farsi typified this.

3. **Inspirational motivation**: the degree to which the leader articulates a vision of greatness that moves followers. Leaders with this orientation continually challenge their followers to attain high standards, communicate optimism about future goals, and give added purpose to the task ahead. There is an energised high sense of purpose, and this is built through effective communication skills. Prophet Muhammad's rapport with Umar ibn Al-Khattab and Khalid ibn Al-Walid reflected this aspect of leadership.

4. **Role and identification model**: this being the apex level of the transformational leadership structure, the leader provides the vision of greatness in tandem with a sense of mission, values and beliefs in action that give ongoing meaning to the task at hand. He gets the active involvement of all stakeholders and leads by example. Together they move in unison. The Prophet's role modeling was closely emulated by Abdul Rahman bin 'Awf and Uthman al-Affan.

Another attendant leadership model that the Prophet of Islam displayed is popularly known in modern management as the Robert Blake and Jane Mouton's **"One-Best Style of Leadership,"** now branded as the Leadership Grid:

Blake & Mouton's The Leadership Grid

High People

1,9 Socialite	Team Leader 9,9
	Middle-of-the-Road 5,5
1,1 Impoverished	Authoritarian 9,1

High Task

which advocates a high task/high people orientation style. The initiators of this leadership model believe that managerial leaders exist to spur efficiency and performance, creativity and innovation, and learning from colleagues. It combines an orientation towards people and an orientation towards results/production While everyone in an organization can ask whereabouts in the grid they should be operating at, the model itself suggests that managerial leaders would best operate at the 9,9 coordinates, where both people and production concerns and interests are fully accommodated. Still, the question remains whether this is always apt, either all the time or at different times.

Both 'concern for results' and 'concern for people' were the main orientations of the Prophet's leadership in the building of a nation state in Madinah.

There is nothing more important in achieving a Vision of Greatness with a Sense of Mission, than by accomplishing it through the conscious wellbeing of people. A good leader does both. An efficacious (efficient as well as effective) leader does whatever it takes to develop the people around him to achieve the desired objective. He does not want to be the socialite 'country-club leader (1,9)' who seeks popularity by being friends with everyone but achieving little in terms of results; nor does he want to be the 'shape-up or ship-out hard taskmaster (9,1)' *sans* compassion. Let alone become the 'impoverished leader (1,1)' who is afraid to create ripples, let alone make waves, thus shunning from taking critical decisions. Neither does he want to be the 'middle-of-the road (5,5)' leader who is half-heartedly mediocre. He should strive to be the *'team leader'* who seeks to achieve excellent results with his people (9,9)!

Even if the leader is now in the 9,9 high-people/high-task category, he should continually carry out a critical self-reflection (*muhasabah*) of his performance orientation to ensure that he does not veer off course in terms of alignment to the commandments of God Almighty. In his endeavours, the Prophet Muhammad had shown that he was the outstanding team leader type.

As an aside, one should perhaps take stock of the sound advice of a pragmatically successful leader, who once reflected:

Everything I need to know about life, I learned from the **Noah's Ark** episode…

1. Make sure you don't miss the boat!
2. Remember that we are all in the same boat, so don't allow anyone to bore a hole in it
3. Plan Ahead! It wasn't raining hard when Noah built the Ark
4. Stay fit. When you're 600 years old, someone may ask you to do something really big!
5. Don't listen to critics, just get on with the job that really needs to be done
6. Build your future on high ground
7. Travel in pairs to ensure greater safety
8. Speed isn't always an advantage. The snails were on board with the speedy cheetahs!
9. When you're stressed, float for awhile
10. Remember, the Ark was built by amateurs, the Titanic by professionals
11. No matter the storm, when you are with God, there's always a rainbow waiting.

Questions to answer from Chapter 3

1. It is imperative for an efficacious leader to have a Vision of Greatness. Please elaborate.

2. Describe briefly what and who is a visionary leader.

3. Describe what and who is a transformational leader.

4. Reflect and discuss what we can learn of leadership from the Noah's Ark episode.

CHAPTER 4

As Manager-Administrator-Diplomat

Once an eminent emeritus professor from the Harvard Business School, Dr Quinn Mills, visited Kuala Lumpur and presented a keynote lecture on the subject of leadership, at the Sunway University College, and asked of the audience "Are you a manager, administrator or leader?"

He posed the question to the audience, and the response by consensus was that one needed to be all three-in-one to be efficacious. Another professor from the University of California Los Angeles (UCLA), Dr Moshe Rubinstein, posed a similar question at the University of Malaya in Kuala Lumpur. The audience surmised that one needed to be three-in-one to be a leader. A manager needs to get results through people come what may; an administrator needs to know the set of rules and procedures by which results are to be achieved; whilst a leader inspires to get the results with (rather than through) his people.

From the study of the *Seerah*, the Prophet Muhammad was all these three-in-one, but he was also a discreet diplomat.

The message of Islam brought to the world by the Prophet Muhammad is holistic, universal and all-encompassing, even when introduced into the micro realms of management and organizational development. Islam is not just puritanical in outlook. The fact that the Prophet gave both spiritual and temporal meaning to life through Islam is testimony of its all-encompassing relevance for all of humankind.

In modern management, we often talk about the global village, sometimes in tandem with the concept of borderlessness. We refer, of course, to the emergence and exponential growth of a free enterprise market system across the globe. It brings forth the outflow of products and services beyond mere national or regional boundaries. This is in consonance with the Islamic paradigm of holistic synergism, meaning that the best is derived from a unified approach of working together for the common purpose in search of a better life, rather than functioning independently of each other.

Thus the mechanisms of the World Trade Organization (WTO), Asia Pacific Economic Cooperation (APEC), Organization of Islamic Conference (OIC), United Nations Development Programme (UNDP), joint space exploration, propagation of green technology, championing of sustainable bio-diversity, the case for a nuclear weapons-free world, and the ethical use of Internet cyberspace for global interactions, all give credence to this view. They provide opportunities and benefits for all people and nations to interact in all fields of endeavour on a daily basis. The Qur'an exhorts this with early messages to all peoples of the world in a universal context:

"Do you not see that Allah has subjected to your (use) all things in the heavens and on earth, and made His bounties flow to you in exceeding measures, (both) seen and unseen? But of the people is he who disputes all about Allah without knowledge or guidance or an enlightening Book (from Him)."

[Qur'an, Lukman, 31:2O]

"…And do not forget your share of legal enjoyment in this world; and do good as Allah has been good to you, and do not seek mischief in the land. Verily, Allah likes not the mufsidun (those who commit great crimes and sins, oppressors, corrupters, mischief-makers…)"

[Qur'an, Al-Qasas, The Narrative, 28:77]

Islamic wisdom's contribution to modern management precludes the temptation of excessive greed and mere focus on profit maximisation. It calls for the altruistic intention (*niyyah*) to do good on earth while continuing to enjoy the bounties provided by Allah the Almighty with magnanimity. This approach emplaces man on a high plane of human consciousness.

"There is enough in this world for every man's need, but not enough for one man's greed."

- Mahatma Gandhi

"For those managers whose aim is to achieve the highest levels of managerial and organizational effectiveness, Islamic wisdom directs them along a road where the pursuit of excellence goes hand-in-hand with their own spiritual development."

- Ron Liamsi

Such an orientation gives managers the opportunity to unravel and assess man's basic humanness as well as historical and cultural similarities. When this opportunity is judiciously put to good use, we would in fact be fusing the real benefits of material progress with those of spiritual fulfilment.

The Prophet Muhammad as Manager-Administrator

While the dichotomy, or fusion, between leadership and management has been an ongoing issue among thinkers and writers, the purpose of this analysis is to adopt the premise that good managers are good leaders because one of the critical functions of management is leading or directing.

Management, as aptly described by Theodore Levitt of Harvard, consists of:

"...the rational assessment of a situation and the systematic selection of goals and purposes (what is to be done?); the systematic development of strategies to achieve these goals; the marshalling of the required resources; the rational design, organization, direction, and control of the activities required to attain the selected purposes; and finally, the motivating and rewarding of people to do the work."

In a large measure, management suggests the use of power in influencing others to attain the predetermined mission or purpose. Leadership, however, caps the whole spectrum of activities mentioned in Levitt's definition by displaying the elements of *competence* and *example*. Leadership in management, or managerial leadership, is about coping with the complexities of the situation at hand.

Good management provides a measure of orderliness and constancy of purpose to key elements of the enterprise: like quality, productivity and profitability. Managerial leadership is also about the ability to initiate and cope with change. Greater change demands a superior quality of leadership. For a start, it needs a measure of good balance between the critical elements of the functions of management and leadership to make things work efficaciously.

"Leaders are people who do the right things, managers are people who do things right."
                                    - Warren Bennis (author/researcher on Leadership)

"Doing things right is not as important as doing the right things."
                                    - Peter F Drucker (management guru)

The chief executive of a corporation, the chief secretary to the government, or even the prime minister of a nation should be able to shift roles and be both manager and leader to be effective. To be efficacious, one needs to be a good managerial leader. Yet the challenge does not end just there. One has to be also a good administrator and diplomat in the quarto-equation.

During Prophet Muhammad's time, it could be said of him that: *"we have in him the characteristic features not only of leadership as a personal quality, but also leadership as an organizational function."* The first feature connotes an extraordinary mix of noble personal traits, whilst the second pertains to the managerial propensity to marshal resources for effective decision-making. It must be remembered that the Prophet Muhammad, whilst being a prophet, was also a man with extraordinary leadership qualities. He was a rational leader who acted with aforethought and judicious calculation, but always benchmarking his actions on the commandments of the Qur'an. And although current research on managerial leadership narrates that there appears to be no specific correlation between a man's ethics and morals against his power to attract followers, yet in his case there existed a distinct correlation between the two factors.

Among the other important things in life, the job of the managerial leader is to reduce uncertainties in his problem-solving and decision-making role. He is usually presented with a set of alternative choices before taking a final decision.

And even if sometimes the leader may not be certain about the preferred choice to make, he must nevertheless take the decision. A leader is not worth his grain of salt if he shuns from taking a decision, however tough it may be. For the valiant, this is when popular traits or characteristics like courage in taking risks, promptness in decision-taking, being calm under pressure, and most of all surrendering to the will of God, find their way to the fore.

It is the first and foremost practice of management to *plan*, for greatness. Whether the aim is to form a team of sportsmen, build an outstandingly competitive organization, or a leading-edge industrial nation, the critical essence is on the function of planning. And God Almighty is, of course, the Greatest Planner. The Prophet of Islam is the embodiment of this fact.

> *"And they planned, and Allah also planned; and Allah is the best of planners."*
> [Qur'an, Al-i-'Imran, The Family of Imran 3:54]

> *"Say, 'Allah is swifter in strategy!'"*
> [Qur'an, Yunus, 10:21]

Traditionally, planning is the management process which is aimed at producing orderly, pre-determined outcomes. The leader with a *vision of greatness* preludes this process with an inductive approach by infusing a sense of direction through a vision-cum–mission statement. Broad strategic goals are then set to achieve a quantum leap effect. Within the ambit of broad goals, quantitative objectives in the form of key result areas (KRAs) and key performance indicators (KPIs) are determined on a periodic basis. The attainment of such goals and objectives is then monitored closely through a just and dependable performance assessment system.

Creating a **Vision of Greatness** requires an inductive, not deductive, approach in the transformation management process. This means that after setting the dateline, we must work our way backwards with the will (*iltizam*) and constancy of purpose (*istiqamah*), by asking ourselves the following strategic questions:

- Where do we want to be? How will we look then? When? (15 - 20 years?)
- How do we get there?
- How do we have to change? What stands in our way?

- What do we actually have to do?
- Who will do what?

It was clear that in the case of Prophet Muhammad, he wanted his Vision of Greatness to be on track. It all started with the well-recounted episode, after his Prophethood, on the little hill of *Al-Safa*, when he called out to the throngs of Quraish: "O people of Quraish, Were I to tell you that an army was advancing to attack you from yonder hills, would you believe me?" "Yes," was the overwhelming answer. "We have always known you to be truthful." Then raising his voice, he called upon each of the Quraish sub-clans, "*O Banu 'Abd al Muttalib! O Banu 'Abd al Manaf, O Banu Zahrah*, I have been commanded by God to warn you, my kinsmen, and I cannot protect you in this world, nor can I promise you aught in the next life, unless you acknowledge that there is no god but Allah."

He was envisioning the greatness of Allah the Almighty, for all to embrace monotheism, rather than falling prey to abject polytheism. Then with a purposeful Sense of Mission, he had conscientiously striven for three long, arduous years to quietly wean his kith and kin away from the worship of idols.

The Prophet of Islam's exhortation towards monotheism, in the Oneness of Allah - as the Vision of Greatness - is supplemented by the mission to create felicity through synergy on earth. This is complemented by a set of goals that are to be achieved by the *ummah* in the message of the last and final *Khutbat al-Wada'*. In the *jihadic* struggle to attain what the Prophet had ordained in the final message from the valley of Arafah, that man will be judged by what he can accomplish by the Prophet's urgings. Such measurements and evaluations are crucial to prove a Muslim leader's success in this world, for the reward in the Hereafter. The Prophet intensely counseled: "I have left among you that which if you hold fast to it, you will not go astray…Allah's book and the *Sunnah* of His Prophet."

The Prophet of Islam's Vision of Greatness Outlook

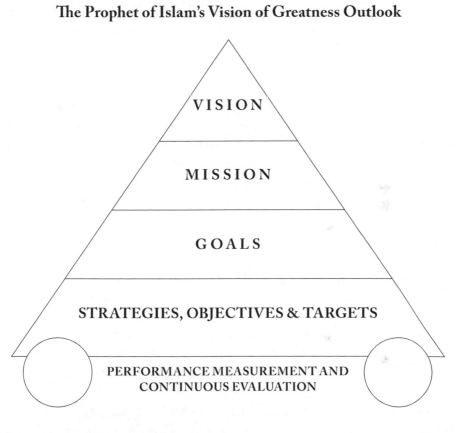

VISION

MISSION

GOALS

STRATEGIES, OBJECTIVES & TARGETS

PERFORMANCE MEASUREMENT AND
CONTINUOUS EVALUATION

The Prophet Muhammad envisioned, with divine guidance, what he wanted to achieve before he undertook the *Hijrah* (Emigration) on July 15, 622AD. This watershed date marked the shift in paradigm from an unsustainable to a meaningfully proactive stance in the administration and propagation of the Islamic law and theology (*Syari'ah*).

One of the critical challenges that a leader faces is the courage to challenge the *status quo* with the hope of inspiring a meaningful transformation of the organization or the nation state.

With the Prophet Muhammad, the change process had begun in his Makkah homeland itself. In his youth, he had already established a reputation for being trustworthy and truthful (*al-Amin*). This splendid sobriquet attributed to him is perhaps best traced to a significant time in 622 AD, while preparing to emigrate to Madinah, and with his life in danger, found the moment to arrange for the return of some items of value earlier entrusted to him for safekeeping.

He was dismayed with the corruption, misery and evils plaguing the society around him. He was appalled by the idolatry and polytheism of the times. He was sickened by the rampant polytheistic beliefs of idol worshippers in Makkah.

In Madinah, Prophet Muhammad played the true manager-administrator role by ordaining the first **Covenant of Aqabah** (*Bait Aqabah*), whereby the early pilgrims from Makkah embraced the Charter promising to worship none but Allah the Almighty, refrain from adultery, stealing and abusing of children; and to observe the teachings of the Messenger of Allah. This mission statement embodied the *Quality Charter* of future delegations of pilgrims. Thus there evolved a set of beliefs that characterised the Muslim *ummah* of Madinah, and later of Makkah.

On the part of the Ansar (the host allies who joyously welcomed him to Yathrib, before being renamed Madinah), they had collectively pledged to him:

"We will obey you, O Messenger of God, in all circumstances, in plenty and in scarcity, in joy and in sorrow, and we will not wrong anyone. We will speak the truth at all times, and we will fear the censure of none in the service of God Almighty."

The Prophet of Islam ensured that the Constitution of Madinah (*Al-Dustur*) organized civic relationships between the various inhabitants of the city state. The aim of the constitutional document was to establish the commitments of each community within Madinah, and define their respective rights, duties and responsibilities. It is believed that there were two parts of the document: (1) the Messenger's peace treaty with the Jewish clans, and (2) the part that explained the commitments, rights and duties of the Muslim populace, comprising the *Muhajirun* and *Ansar*.

Already during the Prophet of Islam's era, there were among the clauses of the constitutional document some key universal principles urged to be practised by modern-day organizations like the United Nations, Amnesty International and Mercy Malaysia:

☐   The God-fearing believers shall be against the rebellious or anyone who seeks to spread injustice, sin, enmity, or corruption between believers; the hand of every man shall be against him even if he is a son of one of them.

◻ God's protection is all-embracing, the least of them may give protection to a stranger on their behalf. Believers are friends and protectors one to the other, to the exclusion of outsiders.

◻ It shall not be lawful to a believer who holds by what is in the document and believes in God and the last day, to help an evil doer or to shelter him.

◻ The Jews of the Banu 'Awf are one community with the believers (the Jews have their religion and the Muslims have theirs), their freedman and their persons except those who behave unjustly and sinfully, for they hurt but themselves and their families.

◻ The Jews must bear their expenses and the Muslims their expenses. Each must help the other against anyone who attacks the people of this document. They must seek mutual advice and consultation, and righteousness is a protection against sinfulness.

◻ The Jews of al Aws, their freedmen and thus themselves, have the same standing with the people of this document and the same loyalty from the people of this document. Righteousness is the protection against sinfulness: each person bears responsibility for his actions. God approves of this document.

◻ This deed will not protect the unjust and the sinner. The man who goes forth to fight is safe and the man who stays at home in the city is safe, unless either has been unjust and sinned.

The Prophet Muhammad was the final arbiter in any contentious situation, and what he had drawn up in this constitution showed the ethical and moral consistencies of Islamic policies, and displayed that Islam did not recognise deceit, treachery and backstabbing.

Apart from ensuring the constitution's sanctity in words and deeds, the Prophet Muhammad guaranteed the just application of the law to all concerned. But the Jews subsequently reneged their side of the deal after some time. They did not merely neglect their duties as defined by the agreed-upon constitution; they also became arrogant and aggressive towards the Prophet despite the fact that they had earlier accepted his leadership according to the terms of the treaty. The Prophet Muhammad had no choice but to expel them from the city-state. This course of action was taken even after the Prophet had gathered the Jews together to advise them of their responsibilities and commitments. When they remained adamant and abusive, the Prophet had no other option but to show them to the door.

Then began the campaigns against the recalcitrant Jews, the most significant being the drive against them in Khaybar – an agricultural oasis, with fertile land and abundant water, and their economic bastion of power. The forces of Islam eventually conquered Khaybar, thereby ending the military and economic power bases of the Jews in the Hijaz region. With the Jews out of the way, the Prophet and his increasing number of followers were free to focus on the job of pacifying the disbelieving Arab tribes and unifying the Arabian Peninsula under the banner of Islam.

The Prophet Muhammad as Diplomat

The peace treaty of Hudaibiyyah had given the Muslims the opportunity to extend their proselytising (*da'wah*) activities in the Arabian Peninsula and beyond. It was reported that among others, the Prophet of Islam had sent Dihyah ibn Khalifah al Kalbi to Caesar, the Byzantine emperor Heraclius; 'Abd Allah ibn Hudhafah al Sahami to Chosroes, the Persian emperor; 'Amr ibn Umayyah al Damari to the Negus of Abbyssinia; Hatib ibn Abu Balta'ah al Lukhami to al Muqawqis, the ruler of Egypt; and Salit ibn 'Amr al'Amiri to Hawdhah ibn al Hanafi in Al-Yamamah. Most of these deputations to kings and rulers of other domains were done between the sixth to the ninth year after the *Hijrah*.

The sending of letters to kings and rulers beyond the Arabian Peninsula was a practical expression of the universality of the message of Islam; which from the beginning in Makkah was authenticated by the following divine pronouncement by Allah the Almighty:

> "*We sent thee not (O Muhammad) but as a mercy to the worlds.*"
> [Qur'an, Al-Anbiya, The Prophets, 21:107]

In *Sahih al Bukhari*, it is quoted that the text of the Prophet of Islam's letter that he dispatched with Dihyah to the governor of Busra (in Syria), who then gave it to Heraclius, was authentically written as follows:

"In the name of God, Most Gracious Most Merciful. From Muhammad, the servant and Messenger of God, to Heraclius, the ruler of Rome:

Peace be upon whoever follows true guidance. I call you to Islam. Become Muslim and be safe, and God will reward you twice. If you refuse, then you will bear the sins of your people. 'O people of the book! Come to common terms as between us and you: that we worship none but God; that we associate no partners with Him; that we erect not, from among ourselves lords and patrons other than God.' If then they turn back, say ye: 'Bear witness that we (at least) are Muslims (bowing to God's will)."

[Qur'an. Al-'Imran, The Family of Imran, 3:64]

It has been authenticated that when the Prophet wanted to write to Byzantium, he was told that the ruler of the empire would not read his letter unless it bore a seal. So he took a seal of silver and engraved it with the words "**Muhammad the Messenger of God – Muhammad Rasul Allah.**" The Prophet thus demonstrated the flexibility of Islamic politics in benefiting from contemporary means and formalities, so long as they did not conflict with the laws and general spirit of the *Shari'ah*.

It will be noted that the letter addressed to Heraclius bore Islamic characteristics. It starts with the *Basmala* (In the name of Allah) and is sincerely forthright in its invitation to the belief in Islam and the prophethood of Muhammad. Simultaneously, it bore the qualities of wisdom, beautiful advocacy, and respect for the addressee ("the ruler of Byzantium"), in view of his standing among his people, encouraging him to embrace Islam – the religion of peace – by mentioning the reward he would receive and warning him of the punishment which would befall him if he kept his people away from Islam.

Al Bukhari referred to the Prophet's dispatching of a letter through 'Abd Allah ibn Hudhafah al Sahami, and asked him to give it to the governor of Bahrayn, Al Mundhir, who then gave it to Chosroes, who in turn mockingly tore it to pieces on reading it. The Prophet supplicated for God Almighty's intervention. God Almighty struck the kingdom of Chosroes to pieces. Chosroes himself was killed by his own son, who ascended his throne. The Persian empire in turn was torn apart and ceased to exist.

The ninth year after the *Hijrah* was named the Year of Delegation *'Am al Wufud* because many delegations from Arab tribes came from all over the Arabian

Peninsula to declare their entry into Islam. It was reported by the *Tabaqat* of Ibn Sa'd that more than sixty delegations pledged themselves to Islam.

In turn, the Prophet first sent deputations outside of Makkah. Khalid ibn al Walid was sent as the governor of Yaman; later he sent 'Ali ibn Abu Talib in his place. Al-Bukhari narrated that 'Ali had succeeded in spreading Islam among the tribes of Hamadan. He stayed there, returning to perform the farewell pilgrimage with the Prophet. Before the farewell pilgrimage, the Prophet had also sent Abu Musa al Ash'ari and Muadz ibn Jabal to Yaman, each one of them administering a province. He exhorted them with the clear message:

"Facilitate things for the people, and do not make things difficult for them. Be kind and merciful with the people, and do not be hard on them, and give the people good tidings, and do not drive them away."
                [Al-Bukhari (Ibn Kathir, *al-Bidayah wa al-Nihayah*, 5/99]

Even when the Prophet Muhammad first came to Madinah, he was faced with hostility and enmity all round. Apart from the loyalty shown by the Ansar allies, the Quraish threatened him from the south, while the tribes of Ghatafan and the Jews of Khaybar were a threat from within. It looked like the whole of the Arabian Peninsula was against him. In his assessment of the situation, Professor Afzalur Rahman in his *Encyclopaedia of Seerah* of the Prophet Muhammad observed it as a tribute to the prophet's political foresight and diplomacy that he was able to handle the various challenges from within and without, one by one, in a remarkable way that within a decade all those opposing forces crumbled, enabling him to become the undisputed leader of the Arabian peninsula. He was the first man to unite all the tribes of Arabia under one rule and give them peace and security. Afzalur Rahman attributed it all to his political skill and diplomatic manoeuvring more than his military strategy and battle successes.

The Prophet Muhammad managed to unite the Arabian Peninsula in less than ten years, despite the strength of the individual spirit and deep entrenchment towards tribal loyalty (*asabiyah*) and ignorant (*jahili*) attitudes. It was a display of ardent unity, strongly entrenched in spirit, mentality and behaviour. Consequently, the Arabian Peninsula became a strong and firm foundation on which the Islamic state would be built, a state whose authority would hold sway, over many areas of Asia, Africa, and Europe.

The Prophet as Holistic Leader

The Prophet Muhammad was the first man who introduced a written constitution of its kind in human history, securing mutual respect, freedom and justice for all citizens of Madinah. The formulation of the *Charter of Liberty* for the city-state embraced all creed, faiths and beliefs. Citizens were guaranteed peace and harmony, while all forms of crime were made illegal. Life and property were guaranteed protection. Security was ensured and preserved. Jews as well as Muslims had freedom of thought and worship. The Prophet, in his capacity as political as well as spiritual leader, created a common defence for the city-state of Madinah from invading hordes and marauders, with the sincere intention of establishing good relations between Jews and Muslims as a united citizenry for a common livelihood purpose.

He displayed outstanding organizational and administrative ability over the Muslim citizenry by enforcing the *Syari'ah* Law. In terms of the well-being of the community (*mu'amalah*), he ensured that food and drinks, social etiquette, trade and commerce, crime and punishment, as well as matters pertaining to morals and ethics, were progressively enforced in accordance with the commandments of the Qur'an. Self-restraint as a quality of life was prescribed through the fast of Ramadan, and the poor were given sustenance by the imposition of tithes (*zakat*) on the wealthier Muslims. For such overtures of magnanimous intent, the Prophet Muhammad was accepted as the *de facto* head of the state of Madinah *al-Munawarah* (Madinah, City of Lights).

The Prophet judiciously used all the political power at his disposal to create and develop the Muslim community and state. And yet, he never exacted forced conversion to display his superior power or deny the right of religious freedom especially of the Jews in Madinah or the Arab Christians of Najran. The Islamisation of the Bedouin pagan tribes in the Arabian Peninsula was done on the basis of genuine concern for basic human rights to be enjoyed by all the Arab communities that come under the protection of the *Khalifah* doctrinaire. The primitive Arab tribes eventually became a contributory part of the bearers of a moderating culture and the builders of civilisation, mainly because of the discipline and rehabilitating effects of Islam. The genuineness of the Prophet's desire to create peace, mutual respect, and cooperation is evidenced by a *hadith*:

"A Muslim is a Muslim's brother. He does not wrong or abandon him. If anyone cares for his brother's need, God will care for his need."

Further, the Qur'an commands, and the Prophet obeys the edict that Muslims should, wherever possible, organise themselves and employ a manner of collective security, including the use of coercion against Muslim elements that seek to disrupt peace and harmony among Muslims:

"And if two parties of believers (or groups) fall to fighting, then make peace between them both. But if one party does wrong to the other, then fight you (all) against the party that is doing the wrong till they return to the commandments of Allah; then if they comply, make peace between them justly, and be equitable. Verily, Allah loves those who are the equitable."

[Qur'an, Al-Hujurat, The Chambers, 49:9]

Where belligerency occurred, it was considered the right of the state to use a measure of force to ensure compliance. Thus for security and harmony to evolve, a good measure of discipline, assertiveness and compliance had to be enforced for the general good of all tribal communities throughout the Arabian Peninsula. And this Prophet Muhammad did to ensure a state of felicity through synergy existed to all and sundry.

Questions to answer from Chapter 4

1. Why is the combination of manager-administrator skills critical for an effective managerial leader?

2. How did the Prophet of Islam manage to expand the Islamic influence to within Arabia and to other nation states beyond the Arabian Peninsula?

3. What did the Prophet Muhammad do to exercise his role as a diplomat and peacekeeper?

4. Describe the Prophet of Islam's role as a holistic world leader.

CHAPTER 5

The Prophet as a Military Commander

The Rationale for War

The many campaigns conducted by the Prophet of Islam constituted a combined strategy to unify the factional tribes of Arabs, Jews, Christians and pagans into an egalitarian populace within the Arabian Peninsula - free of strife, crime and mischief. The sword was used as a symbol of unity, rather than as the misperceived weapon of war.

As a military commander, the Prophet Muhammad was agile, creative and precise in his planning and operational thrusts. He usually led the ranks from the front as per the role of the *amir* in a congregation. The Prophet's own competencies are highlighted through his personal execution of some 27 military campaigns, the building of a city-state at Madinah, and the establishment of diplomatic relations with dominant foreign powers.

The Prophet of Islam's military campaigns demonstrated a unique example of humane warfare, using the minimum show of force wherever possible. They showed clearly the principle of creating the least amount of disruption in society as a consequence of war and war-like situations. As the supreme commander, he never pursued a scorched-earth policy wherever he campaigned and conquered, quite unlike some other iconic conquerors in history who destroyed whatever was before them, in ruthless fashion. The Prophet was a conqueror with great passion and generous compassion.

Sir William Muir, in his writings on 'The Life of Mahomet,' commented that it was strange yet true that the Prophet of Islam succeeded in befriending while defeating his enemies, because he rarely pursued the enemy to the ground after he had tendered timely submission upon the opponent. His commanding appearance inspired the foreigner with an undefined and indescribable awe, but on closer understanding angst and fear gave way to confidence and love.

As commander-in-chief of the Muslim armed forces, he had taken pains to induce the spirit of compassion among his followers, continually reminding his rank-and-file foot soldiers to abide by strict moral and ethical values in times of victory on the battlefield. In modern times, well-known military commanders like Field Marshall Montgomery in his book, 'The Path of Leadership,' described that a good general is not merely one who wins battles; they must be won with a minimum loss of life…when the situation favours boldness."

Retired Brigadier Guzlar Ahmad in his book thesis about 'The Battles of the Prophet of Allah,' conducted within the Arabian Peninsula were the least costly in terms of the loss of human life, in the context of the whole history of wars. He analysed the Islamic nation-state of Madinah expanded its borders at the average rate of 274 square miles per day, over a span of nine years, at the cost of less than 150 human casualties, excluding the campaign at Mowta.

Such minimal cost of human lives was only possible because the objective of going to war was to bring about lasting peace to his homeland and to the world outside, through the spread of the new way of life called the *Ad-Din*. The Prophet's mission of conveying the divine message to humanity in the establishment of peace, with justice and equity, demanded that humanity and human life be protected and saved in order to make good the message entrusted to him by Allah, the Supreme Creator. The object of war was to secure peace, stop injustices and end the exploitation and persecution of people. The legitimacy of going to war was based on two considerations only:

√   when a nation or its people were attacked and their lands and property seized, and

√   when a weak people, whether Muslims or non-Muslins, were being exploited and persecuted by a much stronger power.

Except for these two conditions, war was not justified, not even for the propagation of faith. Compare this with modern-day situations, when whole nations and peoples are put to risk by invasions, bombings and genocidal acts that cause catastrophic disasters of the greatest magnitude, more often carried out for bestial reasons of lust, power and greed.

A military historian and distinguished adjunct professor, Richard A Gabriel, at the Department of History and War Studies at the Royal Military College of Canada in Kingston, Ontario, Canada, in his book 'Muhammad – Islam's First Great General' wrote that Prophet Muhammad was truly a great general, a military theorist, organizational reformer, strategic thinker, operational-level combat commander, political and military leader, heroic soldier, revolutionary, and inventor of the theory of insurgency.

Allah commands that there was to be no use of force – physical, economical, or psychological – in the propagation of Islam.

> "*There shall be no compulsion in (acceptance of) the religion.*"
> [Qur'an, Al-Baqarah, The Cow, 2:256]

However, when situations justify under the two conditions stated above, war became a religious duty, an act of piety. And yet it should be conducted within the parameters set by Allah:

"And fight in the path of Allah those who fight you, but transgress not the limits. Truly, Allah likes not the transgressors."
> [Qur'an, Al-Baqarah, The Cow, 2:190]

Islam began its history not by outlawing wars, but by restricting it to the deterrence of transgressions and aggressions and the defence of the oppressed. This was the kind of legacy left by the Prophet Muhammad.

When a people is invaded, bullied, and oppressed, Allah exhorts:

"And what is wrong with you that you fight not in the cause of Allah, and for those weak, ill-treated and oppressed among men, women, and children, whose cry is: 'Our Lord! Rescue us from this town whose people are oppressors; and appoint for us from You one who will protect, and raise for us from You one who will help."

[Qur'an, An-Nisa', Women, 4:75]

After laying the foundation for the setting up of a nation-state, the Prophet had to plan raising an army for the defence of Madinah against incessant external threats. He had to ensure the training of leaders for the high command of the defence forces, including also for intermediary and junior posts. He had to coach and counsel his subordinate ranking officers on the concept of war in accordance with the fundamentals of Islam. His patience, forbearance, just and fair temperament, and a natural flair for man-management carried the day for the head of state and commander-in-chief.

War, whenever conducted by the Prophet of Islam, was inevitable because it was enjoined upon him by God Almighty, for the emancipation of mankind. It was never carried out to inflict collateral damage. The Prophet was very successful in his military strategies, achieving one success after another, usually against heavy odds. He himself used to organize the expeditions, at critical times leading the campaigns himself. After each military victory, he would decide how to deal with the defeated sides, always showing regard for the just and fair rules of war and peace. Never did he pursue a scorched-earth policy, as said of Prophet Muhammad. Afzalur Rahman observed that one of the greatest contributions of Prophet Muhammad to the civilization of mankind was his civilized laws of war. He purified uncivil and barbaric war customs and traditions of nations and replaced them with the humane, just and benevolent international laws relating to war.

The main principles of Prophet Muhammad's war conduct were:

1. Obedience to the leader (*qa'id*). He laid heavy emphasis on discipline and sound leadership, in order to avoid chaos and defeat.
2. Based on the Qur'anic injunctions, he emphasised the need to meet all obligations and fulfil all covenants, treaties, and pacts with others, irrespective of potential gain or loss involved.

3. Any declaration of war was not unilateral. It was only done when the other party violates or breaks the terms of the treaty, and when notice of retaliation had been served.
4. The modern concept of a surprise attack, *blitzkrieg*, or unilateral declaration of war was not favoured.
5. Peace is always preferred to war, which was only a last recourse. Islam is a religion of peace, and not a religion to pacify at the mercy of the sword. The Prophet Muhammad abided strongly by this principle. He would only resort to war if there was aggression or persecution, particularly when the enemy openly affronts the faith of God Almighty.
6. The Prophet made it a point to treat all prisoners of war with kindness, magnanimity and decorum, and thereafter freed them. In the 13 years of adversarial relationship with the Quraish in Makkah, he and his followers were harshly treated. They even pursued him with grave hostility when he emigrated to Madinah. Yet he never retaliated with vengeance.

Noted scholar and author, Mohammad Marmaduke Pickthall, in his treatise, 'The Meaning of the Glorious Koran,' analytically depicted the Prophet of Islam's achievements as a military leader and strategist. He analysed that the number of campaigns which the Prophet of Islam led in person during the last ten years of his life was 27, in 9 of which there was hard fighting. The number of expeditions which he planned and sent out under other leaders was 38. He personally controlled every detail of the organization, judged every case and was accessible to every supplicant. In those 10 years he destroyed idolatry in Arabia, raised the woman from the status of a chattel to complete legal equality with man, effectually stopped the drunkenness and immorality which had until then disgraced the Arabs, made men in love with faith, sincerity and honest dealing, transformed tribes who had been for centuries content with ignorance into people with the greatest thirst for knowledge, and, for the first time in history, made universal human brotherhood a fact and principle of common law. And his support and guide in all that work was the holy Qur'an.

The Spirit of Jihad

Again, Islam has on many an occasion been misinterpreted by many, even by some Muslims themselves, as 'the religion of the sword,' which is the conduct of *jihad* as a holy war against the disbelievers. Islam is regretfully depicted as a militant theology, like orthodox Marxist-Leninism, bent on world domination to bring about the subjugation of the non-Muslims and others not in sync with its teachings. In modern times, the word has singularly been associated with holy war to defend the sanctity of Islam. This misconception seems to spring from associated terms like *ummah* (the world community), *Dar al-Islam* (where Muslims predominate and where *Shari'ah* law prevails), and *riba* (usury).

Truly, Islam envisages a world order which is a commonwealth of nations, accepting racial diversity and ever-changing geographical demarcations, whilst not constraining the social horizon of its followers. The Qur'an clearly states:

"O mankind! We have created you from a male and a female, and made you into nations and tribes that you may know one another, not that you may despise (one another). Verily, the most honourable of you with Allah is that who is the most righteous of you..."

[Qur'an, Al Hujurat, The Chambers, 49:13]

The purpose of *jihad* is to spur an inward struggle to achieve excellence in oneself and in the process strengthening oneself by correcting one's mistakes. *Jihad* really implies an obligation on the part of Muslim leaders to spread the message of the Islamic concept of an international world order based on the principles of justice, equality and fair play. The true spirit of *jihad*, quite apart from the waging of a holy war, is well explained by Abu Sulayman in his writings that for man to carry out his responsibility as the custodian vicegerent of Allah on earth, he has voluntarily to exert his utmost effort to bring his behaviour in line with guidelines revealed in the Qur'an and *Sunnah* to man by Allah, the Creator and Sustainer of the whole universe. The exertion of the self in all directions, in every effort and act, personal and collective, internal and external, is the essence of *jihad*...in the Islamic sense. Clearly *jihad* is supposed to run through all phases of a Muslim's life as it is his duty in every possible way to do good to the world and prevent harm."

The Military Campaigns led by Prophet Muhammad

Prophet Muhammad, in all of the 27 military campaigns that he led from the front as commander-in-chief, perhaps the three most written about and discussed military battles from the annals of his *Seerah* are:

- The Battle of Badr
- The Battle of Uhud, and
- The Battle of Khandaq

Among the several military campaigns conducted by the Prophet of Islam, these three momentous *ghazawah* each has a lesson of its own for Muslim leaders in time memorial.

Battle of Badr

Badr is a unique landmark in Islamic history. If we recount the *Hijrah* of the Prophet as the beginning of Islam in the pursuit of *Ad-Din* or a new code of life, Badr can claim to be the inspiration to a new lease of life to the mind, body and soul of the Muslim individual. It transformed the human being of the time as being spiritually superior to any other creation. His mental prowess reached new heights and his bodily feats rose to the level of super humans.

The Muslims, for strategic and security reasons, had been monitoring the movements of the trade caravans of the Quraish. The Muslims had adopted a proactive strategy of being on the lookout for Quraish caravans plying the trade routes. One day, the Prophet got news that a large caravan, under armed escort of up to 40 men, led by Abu Sufyan Sakhr ibn Harb, was making its way back to Makkah from Syria. The Muslims drew a plan to confront and seize the caravan as booty. But Abu Sufyan got wind of the plan, detoured by taking another route, and summoned the Makkan leaders to unite and attack the Muslims.

The Battle of Badr took place on Friday, the 7th of the month of Ramadan 2 A.H. The disbelieving Makkan force outnumbered the Muslims by around three to one. The Muslims sent its force to Badr with 319 men against a Quraish force of reportedly 1,000, comprising 950 fighters, with 200 horses, accompanied by singers beating drums, and singing songs insulting the

Muslims. The Quraish armed forces were well sponsored by the wealthy in Makkah and were logistically well-equipped. Their purpose was then to punish the Muslims in order to foil any future Muslim interceptions of their trade routes.

When the Prophet of Islam consulted his Companions and the *Ansar* hosts at his new headquarters in Madinah, he obtained the *iltizam* (total commitment) of his devoted followers to courageously challenge the Quraish offensive, despite the overwhelming odds. The Prophet often engaged in consultation with his Companions and close lieutenants on matters pertaining to situations on which there was no direct revelation in the Qur'an. He did so in order to accustom them to thinking about the general but many problems that affected the security and welfare of the *ummah*, training them to be responsible and accountable on their own. He also wanted to put into practice God Almighty's command on the process of *syura* (consultation). Thus, when approaching Badr, the Prophet organized them: he gave the white standard to Mus'ab ibn 'Umayr; and two black flags to 'Ali ibn Abu Talib and Sa'd ibn Mu'adh. He also placed Qays ibn Abu Sa'sa'ah at the head of the rear guard.

Badr is a place situated near the Red Sea coast, about 95 miles to the south of Madinah. The *Mushrikun* or unbelievers dispatched a spy to find out the numerical strength of the Muslim force heading there. On the day of the Battle of Badr, the Prophet himself organized his army in ranks, ready for the frontal assault. This was a new method of fighting, which differed from the Arabs' normal method of 'attack and retreat,' which the Quraish used at Badr. The creative system of arranging his outnumbered soldiers in ranks enabled the Prophet to reduce the number of casualties among the Muslims, thus also making up for their lack of numbers compared to the enemy's superior numerical strength. The added advantage lay in the fact that the Muslim force was visibly under the control of the supreme commander. He was able to protect the rear of the army, and in this tactical position the leader always had contingency back-up soldiers at the rear to deal with any exigencies.

On the suggestion of Sa'd ibn Mu'adh, a booth was set up for the Prophet so that he could direct the battle campaign from it. When the Quraish force approached the meagre Muslim army, the Prophet inspired and motivated his men, quoting the Qur'an:

"Be quick in the race for forgiveness from your Lord, and for a garden whose width is that (of the whole) of the heavens and of the earth, prepared for the righteous."
[Qur'an, Al-'Imran, The Family of Imran, 3:133]

Facing the attack, the Prophet Muhammad supplicated absorbedly and God Almighty responded,

"Remember you implored the assistance of your Lord, and He answered you: 'I will assist you with a thousand of the angels, ranks upon ranks."
[Qur'an, Al-Anfal, The Spoils of War, 8:9]

So the Prophet briskly came out of the battle booth, declaring:

"Soon will their multitude be put to flight, and they will show their backs (in retreat)."
[Qur'an, Al-Qamar, The Moon, 54:45]

The Prophet Muhammad himself took part in the thick of the battle, The fighting began with the individual combat. 'Utbah ibn Rabi'ah, followed by his son al-Walid and brother Shaybah, from the ranks of the Quraish, came forward and issued a challenge. Some of the young men of the *Ansar* bravely went forward to meet the *Mushrikun*, who shunned and demanded to fight with some of their own people among the Muslim ranks instead. The Prophet then instructed Hamzah, 'Ali and 'Ubaydah ibn al-Harith to fight them. Hamzah managed to slay 'Utbah; then 'Ali killed Shaybah. 'Ubaydah confronted al-Walid, and they wounded each other. Then 'Ali and Hamzah came to 'Ubaydah's aid and killed al-Walid, and carried 'Ubaydah back to the Muslim camp.

The result of the singles hand-to-hand combat depressed the Quraish tremendously, and in the chaos they launched a haphazard general attack. The Prophet responded by ordering his lead Companions to use their bows and shoot arrows at the advancing enemy lines. To get maximum advantage from the flight of the arrows, the Prophet shouted out to his ranks, "When (your foes) come nigh unto you, shoot at them, but use your arrows sparingly."

The Companions 'Urwah and Qatadah mentioned that at close quarters the Prophet flung dust pebbles into the faces of the enemy:

"When thou threwest (a handful of dust), it was not thy act, but God's: in order that He might test the believers with a good test: for it is He Who heareth and knoweth (all things)."

[Qur'an, Al Anfal, The Spoils of War, 8:17]

The two armies engaged in fierce combat during which a number of the *Mushrikun* chiefs were killed, and they included Abu Jahl and 'Amr ibn Hisham, whom the Prophet described as 'the Pharaoh of this nation.' Some young foot soldiers in the Muslim army declared that they wanted to slay Abu Jahl because he had insulted the Prophet, and it was Ibn Mas'ud among them who finally killed the idolater.

Another *Mushrik* leader who was killed was Umayyah ibn Khalaf, who had tortured Bilal in Makkah. The *Ansar* had got wind of this and they killed Umayyah and his son during the campaign.

Among the *Mushrikun*, 70 were killed and 70 were captured. Some of them fell in the places where the Prophet had told his Companions before the battle that they would fall. The enemy forces eventually fled without turning back, leaving a substantial amount of booty on the battleground in Badr.

There are divine *sahih* reports that God Almighty had commanded the angels to help the Muslim army in the Battle of Badr. The wisdom of dispatching angels did not refute the fact that the real fighting action was carried out by the Prophet and his Companions. The angels were merely sent to help them, as reinforcements for the army, taking into account the means and laws which God has set for His creation. God Almighty is the force behind all actions, and indeed He knows best.

☐ **Battle of Uhud**

This battle took place as a result of the attack which the Quraish launched on Madinah, less than a year and one month since their defeat at Badr. The Quraish attack at Uhud was aimed at avenging their defeat and as a retribution for those who were killed at Badr. It was also to wrest back the control of the trade routes to Syria from Muslim hands and to restore the Quraish's high standing among the Arabs.

The Quraish had been preparing for this onslaught since they lost at Badr, and vengeance was on their mind. In this mission, they had also included some women. They number some 3,000 men, with 200 mounted on steed, and 700 in armour. The *Mushrikun* army composed of Quraish combatants and their followers from Kinanah and the people of Tihamah. Khalid ibn al-Walid (before he became a Muslim) led the Quraish troops on the right flank and Ikrimah ibn Abu Jahl on the left.

The books of *Seerah* agree that the battle of Uhud occurred in the month of *Shawwal* in the third year of the *Hijrah*. The exact date is still in contention, but it was said to be on a Saturday in the middle of that month.

This fight is known by the name of the mountain on which it took place, north of Madinah, some 5 kilometres from the Prophet's mosque. The mount of Uhud is made up of red granite rock with many summits. To the south, it faces a small mountain named 'Aynayn, which after the battle was known as *Jabal al-Rumah* (the Mountain of the Archers). Between the two mountains is a valley known as *Wadi Qanah*.

The Prophet had initially thought of defending Madinah from within the fortifications of the city-state in order to minimise the losses of the defenders while maximising the losses of the attackers. It would also utlilise the energies of the entire population, even those who were unable to fight but would like to contribute in the campaign. There was a substantial number of motivated people who had missed out on the Badr campaign and there were those who wanted to display their courage and bravery in the defence of their new faith. But as explained earlier, on consultation with his Companions, the Prophet relented to the view that women, children and the sick would be endangered if the Muslims were to defend Madinah from within.

In spite of the fact that he knew that he had the full protection of Allah the Almighty, the Prophet donned two suits of armour. He did so to show the *ummah* that in any situation, especially the critical ones, they should adopt all available material and physical measures, and having done so, place their full trust in God Almighty.

The Muslim army, as in Badr, was outnumbered. This time around, they had 1,000 men with 100 men in armour, and only 2 horses. But some 300 who initially pretended to be of the Muslim faith withdrew on the pretext that they had only wanted to fight from within the ramparts of Madinah. This act by the hypocrites (*Munafiqun*) was, however, a blessing in disguise as it enabled the Muslims to cleanse their ranks of infidels, who might seek to discourage and influence the half-hearted among the troops.

Indeed, initially the behaviour of the *Munafiqun* had influenced two groups of Muslims, who considered returning to Madinah, but they later held their ground, fought and overcame their lack of confidence with the help of God Almighty.

The Qur'an testified,

"*Remember two of your parties (Banu Salamah* from *al Khazraj* and *Banu Harithah* from *al Aws) meditated cowardice, but God was their protector.*"
                    [Qur'an, Al-'Imran, The Family of Al-'Imran, 3:122]

The Muslim army advanced into the battlefield area of Uhud, taking up positions based on the precise plan of the Prophet of Islam when structuring the ranks of his armed personnel. He situated them in a position facing Madinah, with their backs to the mountain of Uhud, putting 'Abd Allah ibn Jubayr in-charge of 50 archers on top of Mount 'Aynayn, opposite Uhud, so as to protect the Muslims from the possibility of the *Mushrik* enemy cavalry surprising them. The Prophet strongly urged them to keep their positions, saying: "If you see the vultures descending upon us, do not leave your positions, and if you see us overcoming the enemy, do not leave your positions." [Rawahu Bukhari].

In this manner, the Muslims managed to gain control of the high points, leaving the valley to the Quraish army, which advanced with its back to Madinah and facing Uhud.

The fighting was intense and many were martyred during the first stage of the fighting, one of them being Mus'ab ibn 'Umayr, who was the standard-bearer and *da'iyah* Islamic instructor. Ali ibn Abu Talib then took the flag. The Muslim force was gaining the upper hand.

Then something unbecoming happened. When the archers saw the enemy being overcome, they turned to 'Abd Allah ibn Jubayr crying out loud, "The booty, the booty! Our companions have won, so what are you waiting for?" To which Abd Allah ibn Jubayr replied, "Have you forgotten what the Messenger of God told you?" They responded, "By God, we are going to join the people and take our share of the booty." So they rushed down collecting the booty, unheeding the earlier instructions of the Prophet to hold ground come whatever.

When Khalid ibn al-Walid saw what was happening, he took the opportunity to outflank the Muslims and approached them from behind. When the *Mushrikun* realised what was happening, they took heart and began fighting once more, surrounding the Muslims on both sides. The Muslim army thus lost their vantage positions and began to fight back without any plan, in the disarray not able to distinguish friend from foe. The Muslims' strength and enthusiasm were of no avail as their fighting became disorganized. They began to fall in battle as martyrs. What was worse, they lost touch with their supreme commander, the Prophet. What was more startling was that a rumour began to spread among them that he had been slain.

It seemed that the Muslims fled because they heard that the Prophet had been killed. What actually happened was that a small hardy group around the Prophet had managed to hold out. He had remained on the battlefield, but did not allow events around him to confuse him. This was the element of his character in all difficult circumstances. He called out to his Companions, as stated in the Qur'an:

"Behold, ye were climbing up the high ground, without even casting a side glance at anyone, and the Apostle in your rear was calling you back..."
                                        [Qur'an, Al 'Imran, The Family of Imran, 3:153]

Indeed, some of the enemy force had reached the Prophet himself, and were within striking distance. With the Prophet were seven of the *Ansar* and two men from the *Muhajirun*. The Prophet asked, "Who will drive them back from us, and will be my companions in *Jannah*? So one by one they fought to bravely defend the Prophet until all seven *Ansar* fell as martyrs. Then Talhah ibn 'Ubayd Allah fought valiantly until his hand was paralysed by an arrow. Sa'd ibn Abu Waqqas also fought fearlessly in front of the Prophet who handed arrows to him, as he was a very famous archer. Abu Talhah al-Ansari had also defended the Prophet with his bow and arrows. It is narrated that Abu Dujanah was defending the Prophet, shielding him with his back until several arrows were stuck in it, and that his eye was injured, but the Messenger of God restored it with his hand and it became the better of his eyes." [Rawahu Muslim].

Despite the Companions' bravery and courageous defence of the Prophet, the Messenger of God himself suffered wounds. He incurred a broken tooth, and received a wound on his face. Blood oozed from it and he wiped it away, saying: "How can a people prosper who have bloodied the face of their Prophet whilst he is calling them to Islam?" In this regard, the following verse in the Qur'an was sent down:

"Not for thee, (but for God), is the decision: whether He turns in mercy to them or punish them; for they are indeed wrongdoers."
                                   [Qur'an, Al 'Imran, The Family of Imran, 3:128]

The Prophet had thought it very unlikely that God Almighty would guide those who had harmed him in such a way, and God reminded him that it was not so unlikely but if He wished to guide them, then the decision was His. So when his hopes were raised that they would embrace Islam, the Prophet said, "O Lord, forgive my people, for they do not know."
[Rawahu Muslim]

Those who died as martyrs did so because of the motive of *niyyah jihad* by fighting in the cause of Allah alone, and not for other motives. Whoever fights for any other reason, however noble in the sight of men, does not die a martyr. The case of a fighter who fought gallantly because of tribal solidarity, but not in the cause of Allah, was destined for hell. On the contrary, 'Amr ibn Uqaysh, who had hated Islam, had rushed to Uhud to join the Muslims, who tried to prevent him from joining but he told them, "I have accepted Islam." He fought until he was severely wounded whereupon he was carried back to his family. Sa'd ibn Mu'adh came to him and said to his sister, "Ask him whether he was fighting for the sake of Allah?" 'Amr had categorically stated, "For the sake of Allah and His Messenger." Then he died and entered *Jannah* (Paradise).

Some of the women who went out to Uhud along with the Muslim army richly deserves mention. Some were wounded, and some brought much-needed water to the wounded. 'Aishah and Umm Salamah brought water to the wounded in the battlefield after the Muslims withdrew. This showed that when necessary, women were permitted to treat and serve the wounded, as long as it was ensured that they would cause no distraction and as long as they were decently attired. They could also fight to defend themselves if the enemy attacked them.

Despite the fact that *qital* or physical fighting is obligatory only for men if the enemy invades Muslim territory, all Muslims - both men and women - must fight in defence of the cause of Allah. At Uhud 70 Muslim warriors were martyred, with 22 of the Quraish killed.

The main lesson in leadership learnt from the Battle of Uhud is that once the leader has drafted the strategic plan and consulted his men on its execution, there should be no deviation by anyone as to the mission's objective. It was a crucial lesson in focused followership. Lack of discipline, greed and over-confidence can result in utter confusion and losses. Uhud was not a disaster as the Muslims were not totally defeated. The Prophet was saved. It was a reversal in fortune. The Muslim forces had learnt the bitter lesson not to deviate from a predetermined action plan, the next time around.

□ Battle of Khandaq (The Trench/Ditch)

The Battle of Khandaq (*Ghazwat al-Ahzab*) took place in the month of Shawwal in the 5th year A.H. as reported by a majority of scholars. This *ghazwah* occurred as a result of the failure of the Quraish to secure the trade routes to Syria. They had inflicted heavy losses on the Muslims at Uhud, but somehow they did not manage to secure them completely. The threat by the Muslims still prevailed because they still mounted expeditions and campaigns against the *Mushrikun* until the negative effects of Uhud were reversed in Madinah and the surrounding desert region. The Quraish started to think of launching a military offensive against the Muslims in order to achieve their objective of destroying them, this time once and for all.

Since the Quraish were not militarily able to accomplish this objective entirely on their own, they enlisted the help of others in an alliance to wage war on the Muslims. They aligned themselves in particular with the expelled Jews of Banu Al-Nadir and the influential tribe of Al-Ghatafan to form a confederated army, and then gathered in Marr al Zahran, which is about 40 kilometres from Makkah. Just as soon as the gathering of the confederates reached the Muslims, the Prophet in his usual way of leading by example, engaged in

consultation with his Companions on what should be the strategy to deal with
the impending attack on Madinah.

Salman al-Farsi suggested digging a ditch or trench in the northern area of
Madinah to connect with Harrah Waqim and Harrah al-Wabarah. This was
the only part that was open to attack from outside. The other areas were already
like a fortress, in which the buildings and palm trees were interconnected,
surrounded by *hurrahs* where it was too difficult for camels and foot soldiers to
tread. The ditch would serve as a barrier that would prevent direct combat, and
would enable the Muslims to inflict heavy losses on the invaders by shooting
arrows at them from behind it.

Nobody objected to the ingenious plan drawn up for the defence of Madinah,
especially when they realised that the number of assembled confederates was
overwhelmingly huge and the lessons of Uhud were still fresh in the Muslims'
minds.

Despite the period of famine and the inclement cold weather, the ditch was
completed in good time. This was due to the faith (*iman*) and their commitment
to work as equals when digging and carrying the soils. The Prophet Muhammad
himself partook in the laborious work, singing songs and poems along with
them in harmony, although covered with dust and grime. He even tied a stone
to his stomach because of extreme hunger.

The fact that the Prophet himself actively participated along with the Muslim
brethren and not just merely giving moral support had a great effect on the
followers' morale and they were further resolved to face the trying times ahead.
A number of miracles happened to the Prophet during the six days of intense
digging and earth-carrying operations, one of which was the multiplication of
scarce food.

The Prophet's companion, Jabir ibn 'Abd Allah, noticing that the Prophet
was suffering from severe hunger, asked his wife to prepare some food for
him. Jabir slaughtered a goat in his meagre flock while his wife grounded a
measure of barley in a small pot. Jabir then invited the Prophet to come and
eat, apologising how little was the food he had prepared. The Prophet in turn
called on the other Muslims to share the food with Jabir. Happily, some 1,000
Muslims came to eat. The Prophet blessed the pot and everyone ate until they

were all satisfied. And yet there was still plenty left in the pot! It was Allah Who had blessed the occasion.

The confederate army had an overwhelming numerical advantage – reportedly some 10,000 warriors and foot soldiers. They had 300 horses and 1,500 camels, and they were further joined by some 700 soldiers from the tribe of Banu Salim. On the Muslim side, the army numbered 3,000 warriors. It was a much better showing than when they fought at Badr when they had only some 300 warriors.

The Quraish forces were perplexed when they saw the ditch dug outside the ramparts of the Madinah city-state. They were at a loss in figuring how they could breach it. Every time they tried to do so, they were showered with arrows. The siege intensified and lasted for at least 14 days. There was no real hand-to-hand combat except for the exchange of arrows. The spirit of the confederate army was eventually eroded because of the lengthy period of the siege; and also because of the influx of a really strong, cold wind into the siege area. God Almighty began to aid the Muslim believers with an east wind, which was so intense that it pulled up the soldiers' tents, turned over their cooking pots, extinguished their fires, and buried their saddlebags in the sands. Their supreme commander, Abu Sufyan, growing very depressed, finally shouted at them to leave camp. Thus the only results they achieved from this *ghazwah* were tiredness and high costs, as stated in the Qur'an:

"O ye who believe! Remember the grace of God (bestowed) on you, when there came down on you armies (to overwhelm you): but We sent against them a hurricane and forces (of angels) that ye saw not: but God sees (clearly) all that ye do."
[Qur'an, Al Ahzab, The Allies, 33:9]

The confederates were exasperated and they helter-skelteredly withdrew from Madinah, never to bother the city-state at close range again.

"And God turned back the unbelievers for (all) their fury: no advantage did they gain; and sufficient is God for the believers in their fight. And God is full of strength, able to enforce His will."
[Qur'an, Al Ahzab, The Allies, 33:25]

Truly, God Almighty had answered the supplication of His Prophet at the time of the siege. The Prophet had expressed his joy at the significant effects of the

Confederates' failure to invade Madinah: "Now we shall invade them, and they will never invade us again. We will go and fight them in their own territory."

[Sahih al-Bukhari]

The significance of Khandaq meant that the Muslim strategy had begun to shift from the defence of Madinah into attack. The arena of events moved from Madinah and its environs to Makkah and Ta'if, then to Tabuk, which was far away from the Islamic city-state of Madinah.

Questions to answer from Chapter 5

1. Describe the Prophet of Islam's role as a Military Commander.

2. Give a short description of each of the three significant wars led by the Prophet of Islam.

3. What is the moral and strategic learning lesson from each of the three significant battles in Islamic history?

CHAPTER 6

The Prophet in the Role of an Economic Leader, Social Master

The term "Economic Leader, Social Master" refers to the leader who assumes the dual roles implied therein. The Prophet Muhammad became both a highly successful businessman and social entrepreneur. Makkah during the Prophet's time was the traditional centre of trade in Arabia.

The underlying ethos of the Arabian Peninsula at the time was that the Quraish, being the custodian of the Ka'abah (Arabic: Cube), were acknowledged as the noblest and most influential of tribes in the region. By count, the number of tribes scattered throughout the whole Arabian Peninsula, totaled almost fifty. The fact that all these tribes accorded their collective respect and honour gave the Quraish three distinct benefits:

1. They had a commanding influence over all other tribes in the region;
2. Their central geographical location facilitated trade and interactions, which placed them in positions of tribute and profit; and
3. Makkah, by Arabian custom, being sacredly protected from the ravages of war and private feuds, had been accorded security by the general populace and was free from the external threats of attack.

Indeed, in the Qur'an, the Quraish were reminded of the blessings and mercy of Allah, in these words:

"(It is a great grace from Allah) for the accustomed security of the Quraish; (and with all those Allah's grace and protections, We cause) the (Quraish) caravans to set forth safe in winter (to the south) and in summer (to the north without any fear), so let them worship (Allah) the Lord of this House (the Ka'bah in Makkah), (He) Who has fed them against hunger, and has made them safe from fear."

[Al-Qur'an, Quraish, The Quraish, 106:1-4]

It was thus appropriate that the Quraish took full advantage of the status accorded to them. They sent their commercial caravans to all the neighbouring states, thus making themselves rich and powerful. With official security and trading permits given by the authorities of the neighbouring states, they dispatched their trading caravans to the north (Syria, Iran and Iraq) during the summer, and in the winter to the south (Yemen and Abyssinia), without any fear of danger or reprisals. For instance, the four sons of Abd Manaf: Hasham, Abd Shams, Muttalib and Naufal, successfully obtained trading permits called *aylaf* (agreements), enabling the Quraish to make substantial strides in commerce and garnering enormous profits.

So also for the enterprising helpless women and orphans, and rich widows, they were given trading opportunities (through *shirkat* or partnerships). The person who provided the capital could either engage in trade himself or choose to enter into partnership and thus a share in both the profit and loss (*mudarabah*) of the business. Saidatina Khadijah herself was a rich widow and conducted her trading activities with different persons on such terms. Muhammad, before his prophethood, had himself begun trading of a commercial nature with her funds, on a partnership basis. The trading business community of the enterprising Quraish tribe flourished by sending their commercial caravans to various states and other areas outside the region all-year round.

Muhammad, when he became the Messenger of God Almighty, brought to humankind the divine guidance in all its details: beginning with *Fard 'Ain* - the Articles of Faith related to *Tawhid* (the monotheistic belief in the Oneness of Allah), the five obligatory prayers, the institution of *Zakat* (poor-due), the *Siyam* (fasting), and the performance of the *Haj* (pilgrimage to Makkah).

Muhammad the Young Business Entrepreneur

In his youth, Muhammad was under the guardianship of his uncle, Abu Talib, who had good faith in his nephew's entrepreneurial flair and honest-to-goodness approach in his dealings. Makkah was an expanding commercial hub. Being an orphan, Muhammad was at a disadvantage if he had wanted to pursue a business profession. Business during that time was interpreted as all transactions that were carried out for profit, gain, benefit, etc., as in trade, commerce, and industry, by which one satisfied the needs of another who pays for the services rendered. Historian Montgomery Watt, when writing about the 'Muhammad: Prophet and Statesman,' raised the question: "In this world of unscrupulous businessmen, how was a poor orphan, however gifted, to make his way?"

Muhammad's main assets, however, were his integrity, honesty, astuteness, moral intelligence and conscientiousness. Muhammad was already tending sheep for shepherds on a small wage in his boyhood. Because he grew up in the house of Abu Talib, a trader, he must have learnt something about trading at such an early age. Evidence seems to suggest that Muhammad in his adolescent years must have started his trading activities on his own, with partners, such as Saib ibn Ali Saib and Qais ibn Saib. As an orphan, he did not want to unduly burden his already financially-stretched uncle over the family budget. For this purpose, he would have ventured into Yemen and its market towns on several occasions as a young entrepreneur, well before his assignments with Khadijah. Muhammad bore the hallmark sobriquet of *al-Amin*, which identified his character traits of honesty, trustworthiness, and acumen.

Trade and commerce would certainly be the better off with these noble traits. The holy Prophet had said: "*Take to trade, because out of ten divisions of livelihood, nine are in trade.*" Hence the reason why the Prophet Muhammad took trade seriously to show others the way how business should be conducted according to the commandments of the Qur'an and his *Sunnah*.

It was when he accompanied his uncle to assist him on some business trips that he displayed such an outstanding entrepreneurial persona. It was on Muhammad's urgings that his uncle Abu Talib one day took his eagerly youthful nephew on a commercial trip to Damascus. It was also during this trip that the young Muhammad was exposed to the full realities and vagaries of trade and commerce. Even from the then tender age of only 12, Muhammad was already showing great aptitude, maturity, power of observation, memory, and all the qualities which God Almighty had bestowed him with. His uprightness, intelligence, charity and warm disposition impressed Abu Talib and his business associates.

Abu Talib, however, was not without constraints in terms of financial resources to go on an expansion of his business interests. Realising this, Muhammad was always looking for ways to help lighten his uncle's burden of having to support a large family.

The Prophet Muhammad as an ideal businessman

Muhammad got the opportunity to expand his horizon in commerce when he was assigned to go on an important business trip to Syria as the steward of a noble Quraish businesswoman named Khadijah binti Khuwailid.

An account by Ibn Sa'd related Abu Talib as having said to Muhammad as follows:

"I am, as you know, a man of scanty means, and truly the times are hard with me. Now there is a caravan about to start for Syria and Khadijah, daughter of Khuwailid, is in need of the services of men of our tribe to take care of her merchandise. If you offer yourself for this enterprise, she would readily accept your services." Khadijah, who had already heard of Muhammad's honesty, trustworthiness, and high moral character was readily prepared to offer him twice what she would have paid to any other capable man of Makkah.

The exact destination of the caravan happened to be Damascus, where Muhammad had earlier been with his uncle. The caravan took the usual route to Syria, the same one which Muhammad had earlier traversed with his uncle, *via* Busra – on the road to Damascus. This time around, Muhammad was accompanied by Khadijah's servant, Maysarah. Along the journey, Muhammad sat down to take a rest under a shady tree. A Christian monk, who lived nearby, on seeing him, rushed to the spot and said, "Right from Jesus, the son of Mary, none ever sat here but a prophet. He is the Prophet, and the last of the Apostles."

Being already familiar with the surrounding trading environment, Muhammad was bent on carrying out his assignment with the utmost sincerity, honesty, trustworthiness, and astuteness. He bought for Khadijah all that she had expected and reaped abundant returns. In spite of the commendable gains he made, Muhammad's prudence and virtuosity in executing the business deals so impressed Khadijah that in time they both drew themselves closer together.

The Prophet undoubtedly undertook a few more trading and commercial trips to various business locations in Syria and Yemen. Khadijah was a notable personality in Makkan society, and after they were both married, Muhammad expanded his realm of duties and activities. He then had to look after his business affairs, take care of his family with children, and undertake further journeys for the expansion of trade and commerce. Yet beyond these, Allah had *plus ultra* or greater things ahead for him. And the beautiful and noble Khadijah, who although was 15 years his senior in age, provided for Muhammad another 25 years of hope and consolation, ease of circumstances, freedom from the mundane chores of daily life, strength and comfort of deep mutual love – the very factors that later contributed to the furtherance of his mission as a Prophet.

Muhammad carried out his business dealings with extreme honesty and fairness, never providing reason for any of his customers to complain. His word was always his bond, whether it involved timely delivery of trade goods, the quality of such goods, or the reasonability of the prices mutually agreed upon.

Among his notable quotes are:

"God shows Mercy to a man who is kindly when he sells, when he buys and when he makes a claim."

[Rawahu Bukhari]

"No one has ever eaten better food than what he eats as a result of the labour of his hands."

[Rawahu Bukhari]

"The truthful and trusty merchant is associated with the prophets, the upright and the martyrs."

[Rawahu Tirmidhi]

After his marriage with Khadijah, Prophet Muhammad still carried on his trading and commercial business, as a full-fledged manager and partner in his wife's expanding business venture. It seems most certain that during his late twenties and mid-thirties, he travelled many times to various trading centres and commercial fairs up and down the country, as well as to the neighbouring countries of Yemen, Bahrain, Syria and Iraq during summer and winter. Three of his commercial journeys after marriage were reported: one to Yemen, the second to Najd, while the third was to Najran. The reporter also narrated that in addition to these expeditions, Muhammad was busily engaged in active trading, during the seasons of the pilgrimage, in the commercial fairs such as at Ukaz, Mushaqqar and Dhul Majaz; and in other seasons, he was also busy conducting his wholesale business in the markets of Makkah.

Only when he was in his late thirties was Muhammad intensely inclined to meditation and devotion. Towards this purpose, he regularly retreated (engaged in *tahannuth* or sojourn) and spent days and sometimes weeks in the cave of Hira' on mount Jabal al-Nur. This huge rock of golden mica is located a few miles to the north of Makkah, glistening in the rays of the glowing sun; yet it is desolate, barren and waterless. Within its rocky side is a small dark cave, where Muhammad spent days, and sometimes nights, eating and sleeping little, before returning home. He would then gather more provisions to ascend the cave for a similar retreat.

Then one day, unexpectedly, the Truth came to him, commanded to "Read," (*Iqra'*) the first word of the Qu'ran he heard: "*O Muhammad, you are the Messenger of Allah!*" (Bukhari, 1:1). It also seemed to him that every stone or tree that he passed by uttered, "*Peace be to you, O Messenger of Allah.*" When he reached home, he told Khadijah the whole episode. Whereupon, Khadijah promptly consulted her cousin, Waraqa ibn Nawfal, a scholar and believer, who affirmed that Muhammad was the long-expected final Prophet.

In retrospect, it was abundantly clear that Muhammad conducted a good deal of business before his prophethood; and it had been witnessed that he was the most ideal businessman, establishing mercantile rules for the prosperity of individuals as well as for a nation. After the divine mission was entrusted upon him by Allah Almighty, his engagements in trading and business activities gradually decreased. Soon after the emigration to Madinah, trading by way of selling trickled almost to a halt although some buying activities still occurred.

Muhammad the Social Entrepreneur *Extraordinaire*

A social entrepreneur is a truly exceptional individual who dreams up and takes responsibility and accountability to convert an innovative and untested vision for positive societal change, from dream into reality, whatever the odds. What enabled a social entrepreneur to make a lasting impact, while facing the most difficult problems and challenges, is a special combination of groundbreaking creativity and steadfast execution.

Social entrepreneurs are individuals with innovative solutions to society's most pressing social problems. They are ambitious and persistent, tackling major social issues and offering new ideas for wide-scale change. They are not only game players; they are also game changers.

Rather than leaving societal needs to the powers-that-be or business sectors, social entrepreneurs find and analyse what is not right by solving the problem and changing the system, sharing the solution, and persuading entire societies to take new quantum leaps. To be a social entrepreneur one must first have the heart and discipline of a social worker, an enabler who helps others help themselves. Being a social worker can be physically demanding and emotionally draining, thus de-stressing is an important aspect of the vocation. In modern times, a social worker works with corporations to help initiate corporate social responsibility (CSR) programmes.

Social entrepreneurs are often seen to be passionate about their ideas, committing even their lives to changing the direction of society's ways of doing things, for betterment. They are both visionaries and ultimate realists, concerned with the pragmatic implementation of their vision of greatness. Every leading social entrepreneur is a change-master who is a mass recruiter of local change-makers – a role model proving that citizens who channel their passion into action can make almost everything possible.

Just as business entrepreneurs change the face of business, social entrepreneurs act as the change agents for society at large, seizing opportunities others overlook and improving systems, innovating new approaches, and creating solutions to change society exponentially. While a business entrepreneur might create entirely new ventures, a social entrepreneur comes up with new solutions to social problems and then implements them on a large scale. They are innovators for the public good.

Prophet Muhammad's contributions in this holistic direction of human affairs are comparatively echoed and displayed by modern social entrepreneurs *extraordinaire* the likes of Bangladeshi's Professor Muhammad Yunus (Grameen Bank), India's Prem Rawat (Prem Rawat Foundation), and Japan's Daisaku Ikeda (Soka Gakkai). Some personalities who are known for their social entrepreneurship outreach are:

- Professor Dr Muhammad Yunus (Bangladesh). Founder of the Grameen Bank, providing micro-credit for especially women small entrepreneurs, who are the mainstay of the rural economy. As a Nobel laureate, his model is emulated the world over.
- Dr Maria Montessori (Italy), who developed the Montessori approach to early childhood education.
- Vinoba Bhave (India), the founder and leader of the Land Gift Movement; he caused the redistribution of more than 7 million acres of land to aid India's landless and untouchables.
- Florence Nightingale (U.K.), the founder of modern nursing; she established the first school for nurses and fought to improve hospital conditions
- Susan B Anthony (U.S.A.), who fought for women's rights in the United States, including the right to control property and helped spearhead the adoption of the 19th Amendment.

In the role of "**Economic Leader, Social Master**," the Prophet Muhammad realised in his time that throughout the whole of the Arabian Peninsula the focal mode of life's activities was centred mainly on trade and commerce, which in modern-day parlance means capitalism, but it became a serious concern when the unequal distribution of wealth created a major socio-economic problem in society. In his boyhood years, Muhammad lacked capital to do business on his own; yet he was able to have access to the ample funds of the wealthy who would welcome any honest trader who could utilise their capital to invest with and bring in good returns on the basis of profit-sharing.

In truth, the Prophet Muhammad engaged in business only to sustain his and his family's basic needs, although through honest business acumen he made good profits and brought substantial returns for his funders. The Holy Prophet was not sent to earth as a tradesman. He had been quoted to have said:

"I have not been given Revelation to hoard up wealth or to be one of the tradesmen."

Yet he had shown the secret of success in business: that by being morally upright and honest in all his dealings and transactions, there will come prosperity that is blessed by Allah the Almighty.

What concerned him much more, however, was the large gaps in both economic and social equality among his people. To begin with, even in socio-economic terms, there were areas of unjustness in the ways business was transacted that needed to be put right. The following are some of the areas of concern that the Prophet Muhammad addressed during his period of leadership in Makkah and subsequently in Madinah:

> Principles of fair trading

He always observed the principles of fair dealing in business transactions: such as avoidance of interest, fraud, exploitation, black-marketing, hoarding, cheating, gambling, dubious profiteering, and uncertainty. In this he exhorted his Companions to do likewise.

To prevent fraud and short-weighing, the Prophet Muhammad standardised weights and measures and forbade traders from using other, less reliable, standards of weighing and measuring.

> Lawful earnings

He showed the way to earning his incomes lawfully, during his boyhood, youth and manhood – beginning in Makkah. He was reported to have said:

"No one has ever eaten better food than what he eats as a result of the labour of his hands. Allah's Prophet Dawud used to eat from what he had worked for with his hands."

[Rawahu Bukhari]

➤   Forbidden businesses

Businesses declared unlawful in the Qur'an include: consumption of flesh of swine, blood, dead animals, or alcohol.

"O you who believe! Eat of the good things that We have provided for you, and be grateful to Allah, if it is Him you worship. He has only forbidden you dead meat and blood, and the flesh of swine and that on which any other name has been invoked besides that of Allah."

[Qur'an, Al-Baqarah, The Cow, 2:172-3]

The prohibition also meant that Allah and His Messenger have declared forbidden the sale of wine, animals which have died a natural death, swine and idols. Prophet Muhammad further declared,

"The price paid for a dog is impure, the hire paid to a prostitute is impure, and the earnings of a cupper are impure."

[Rawahu Bukhari and Muslim]

➤   Good conduct in business dealings

Conduct in business can at times get unruly and uncouth, especially during contentious moments of disagreements. The Prophet Muhammad himself was always very gentle and respectful in his business transactions, and he counseled his Companions to be likewise. Jabir reported Allah's Messenger as having said

"Allah's mercy to a man who is kindly when he sells, when he buys, and when he makes a claim."

[Rawahu Bukhari]

Then he added,

"Avoid much swearing while transacting business, for it produces a ready sale, (but) then blots out the blessing."

[Rawahu Bukhari & Muslim]

➤ Rights of parties in transactions

Allah and His Messenger have made the exchange of goods, with mutual consent of the parties in trade transactions, legal and lawful, and have forbidden people from taking other people's things without their consent and permission. This was necessary for maintaining peace and order in society and for keeping cordial relations between the various members of the community. However, the Prophet Muhammad also laid down certain rules and conditions for such transactions, and gave each party the right to keep or break the transaction. Hakim ibn Hizam reported Allah's Messenger as having said:

"Both parties in a business transaction have a right to annul it so long as they have not parted; and if they tell the truth and make everything clear they will be blessed in their transaction, but if they conceal anything and lie, the blessing on their transaction will be blotted out."

[Rawahu Bukhari & Muslim]

➤ Clean business transactions

The Prophet Muhammad was sent by Allah to cleanse society of all that is unhealthy, unclean and immoral whether of things and ideas, and generate pure things and ideas instead. "Pure things" imply that they should be wholesome, and must have been earned in lawful ways. The Prophet explained:

"Allah is good (and pure) and accepts only good (and pure) things, and He has given the same command to the believers as he has given to the Messenger."

➤ By mutual consent

The Qur'an commands Muslims to conduct their business affairs by mutual consent of the parties concerned. Mutual consent implies that the transactions need to be carried out by mutual or reciprocal understanding and agreement, and not by coercion or fraud.

> *"O believers, do not devour one another's property by unlawful means; do business with mutual consent."*
>
> [Qur'an, An-Nisa', Women 4:29]

In the context of the commandments of Allah, and as explicitly stated in the Qur'an, the Prophet Muhammad laid down the rules and regulations for all types of business transactions. Thus the forms of business transactions that did not fulfil the conditions laid down, were deemed unlawful. He promoted the life pursuit of living in moderation, which has become the golden mean of Islam. By his very example, he transformed the socio-economic system of the community at large throughout the Arabian Peninsula, in order to bring light to darkness.

Corporate Social Responsibility (CSR)

The Prophet Muhammad had clearly initiated business practices in line with responsible, ethical, and virtuous social behaviour. As an entrepreneur and trading agent since even his boyhood days, the Prophet had shown consistent ethical, moral and social behaviour. He made it a point to make social responsibility an intrinsic part of both his personal and business activities. This was evident especially when he was helping his uncle Abu Talib and then the noble businesswoman *Saidatina* Khadijah in trade and commerce.

In the modern context, Corporate Social Responsibility (CSR) has become the benchmark in the business environment of the more civilised societies to ensure the development of a more responsible and sustainable set of business practices that can benefit both the corporation and the community at large. Economic, social, human rights and environmental considerations are to be given priority beyond mere profit motives. The irony of it is that people who do business by embracing the spirit of CSR tend to make more profits because they encourage innovation and customer loyalty. Being a better corporate citizen is a source of competitive advantage, with fewer business risks, avoiding consumer boycotts, being better able to obtain capital at a lower cost, being in a better position to attract and retain committed employees, and building a much improved customer loyalty base. The challenges are many, just as the Prophet of Islam faced numerous obstacles during his time. Yet, he prevailed, and over a period of 23 years, he managed to execute and transform exponential change.

In the 10 years the Prophet Muhammad administered Madinah, the system of *Mu'akhah* (mutual brotherhood), the strengthening of the bonds of faith between the emigrant *Muhajirun* and hosts *Ansar*, developing love among the populace as the foundation of society, and building the bridges between rich and poor all began to take shape. The environment was cleansed physically and spiritually.

In recent times (mid-May 2010), one of the world's most tragic environmental disasters (and certainly the worst in the USA) happened in the Gulf of Mexico, where oil giant British Petroleum's operator was reportedly responsible for the substantial catastrophic oil leak that at one time spewed out some 19,000 barrels a day from the deep-water wells to the gulf's surface (compared to a previous disaster of 5,000 barrels a day during the Exxon Valdez oil spill in Alaska). After 100 days since the oil slick from the Gulf of Mexico spill it was reported that from as low as 5,000 feet below the earth's surface, some 5 million barrels of crude oil had spilled outwards, causing massive environmental disaster that was estimated to last a decade.

The US Federal government was left hamstrung because initially the BP corporate leadership had not really grappled with the situation hands-on until the seventeenth day of the disaster when, under severe criticism, it forced the personal intervention of President Barack Obama. He took direct responsibility and accountability and paid hands-on visits to New Orleans, Louisiana to oversee the situation. The people of Louisiana had earlier in the past suffered the wrath of hurricane Katrina, when at that time President George W Bush was reported to be heavily criticised for acting too late to address the situation.

The state's local population, a sizeable portion of whom depended on the fishing industry, was left high-and-dry, with small coastal business owners condemning BP for putting profits before lives. Eleven human lives were lost during the initial days of the oil platform explosion. Wildlife casualties and rehabilitation efforts were enormous. The oil leak had destroyed the area's wetlands and pristine waters of the gulf. In spite of the technological achievements in the most advanced nation, a lot remained to be desired.

Clearly, we need to see more world leaders operate from the heart, especially in modern times when the dominance of greed, hedonism, and material wealth have taken its toll on the global populace.

So, on the socio-political scene, much more need to be done to pay heed to God Almighty's commandment to sustainably protect and prosper the earth we live on.

Questions to answer from Chapter 6

1. What is meant by the term "Economic Leader, Social Master?"

2. How did Prophet Muhammad play the role of Economic Leader?

3. How did the Prophet Muhammad play the role of Social Master?

4. What made Prophet Muhammad a highly successful businessman?

5. Discuss the importance of social work and social entrepreneurship in developing a civil society.

CHAPTER 7

The Seven-Step Process of Managing Change

Transformation involves the process of change. The Seven-Step change process (SADPAAI) sequence developed by the Prophet Muhammad is as follows:

1. S = Survey
2. A = Approach
3. D = Diagnose
4. P = Plan
5. A = Act
6. A = Appraise
7. I = Institutionalise

1. Survey

Even before his prophethood, Muhammad was very worried and disturbed by the disparaging way of life prevailing at the time in Makkan society. He surveyed the environment around him and found ignorance (*Jahiliyyah*) to be the order of the day. The people of Makkah were practising rampant polytheism, especially at the Ka'abah. He longed for the monotheistic stance of his spiritual forefathers Ibrahim and his son Ismail. As a young man and until he attained the prophethood at 40 years old, Muhammad had consciously distanced himself from the frequent tribal ritualistic ceremonies held in the precincts of the Ka'abah.

He loathed the habitual alcoholic drinking sessions amidst the intermittent wild gambling scenes. He abhorred the frequent factional wars among the Makkan clans, sometimes over trivial matters of pride and prejudice. He could not fathom the cruelty of fathers who killed their newly-born daughters.

Thus, it was not surprising that Muhammad retreated to the solace of the cave of Hira' on mount Jabal al-Nur to reflect on how to overcome the ignorance and sins of his people. In the solitariness of a cave, he meditated and searched for the inspiration that would bring everlasting harmony to his homeland.

> *"And He found you wandering, and gave you guidance."*
> [Qur'an, Ad-Dhuha, The Early Hours, 93:7]

On attaining prophethood, Prophet Muhammad totally committed himself to pursuing Allah the Almighty's commandments and guidance to transform the prevailing pathetic state of affairs in Makkan society from darkness to enlightenment.

2. Approach

To begin with, who could the Prophet Muhammad turn to for help to promote his divine cause? Based on his survey of the environment, the Prophet of Islam began to question and fathom who among his closest relatives, Companions and friends could commit themselves to the faith of the One and Only God Almighty.

Historian Edward Gibbon described that "the first and the most arduous conquests of Mahomet were those of his wife, his pupil, his servant and his friend (namely Khadijah binti Khuwailid, Ali ibn Abi Talib, Zaid ibn Thabit and Abu Bakr As-Sadiq); since he presented himself as a Prophet to those who were most conversant with his infirmities as a man." And nobody can be more aware of the frailties of a man than his own beloved wife, Khadijah, who at the time had already been married to the Prophet Muhammad for 15 years, and was still going strong. It was natural, therefore, for Khadijah to be the first to commit herself unreservedly to the voice of prophecy. These were the people close to the Prophet who formed the core of *tanzim haraki* or purpose-driven team, propagating the religion of Allah. Initially, for a period of three years, the Prophet propagated the Oneness of Allah and righteous ways of living, in secret.

3. Diagnose

In Makkah, the Prophet Muhammad and his core of followers were incessantly confronted with threats, abuses, and even physical torments, all in the cause of Allah. He noted the severe resistance and hostilities posed by the vengeful Makkan leaders, especially from the opposition leader Abu Jahl and later from the Prophet's own uncle, Abu Lahab. The poor and the weak among the Prophet's followers were markedly persecuted. Bilal, Ammar ibn Yasir and Khabbab, to name a few, were tortured and at times inhumanly treated by their disbelieving masters.

From around the year 616AD, the Prophet's followers who constituted the clan of Bani Hashim were boycotted for three straight years, and exiled to the outskirts of Makkah, without adequate food, water or proper shelter. In the interim, he lost his beloved wife Khadijah and his uncle Abu Talib, who both passed away.

The Prophet's trip to the neighbouring hillside town of Ta'if for support and compassion was met with further ridicule, insults and injuries hurled at him. Having secured the protection of the leader of another clan, the beleaguered Prophet returned to Makkah.

Of such severity were the pangs of hate and campaigns of profanity conducted by the polytheistic disbelievers that the Prophet of Islam had to make serious contingency plans for the safety and well-being of some of his more stricken followers.

A selected few were encouraged to emigrate to the safe haven of Abyssinia, where the Christian king there – after hearing out the visitors' explanations of the faith they have brought and sensing its comparative likeness to his own faith - showed sympathy towards the persecuted followers of the new religion of Islam.

4. Plan

The *Covenant of Aqabah*, by which provisions a representative party of 87 converted Madinans accorded their collective loyalty, respect and safety to the Prophet Muhammad and his followers, was activated.

On hearing of a plot by the Makkans to assassinate him, the Prophet unfolded a plan to urge his followers, about 70 in all, to emigrate to friendly Yathrib (later renamed Madinah) in small groups.

The plan was to set up the base for a new Islamic stronghold in the city-state of Madinah. Having his confidante Ali Abi Talib as his decoy in Makkah, the Prophet and his chief lieutenant Abu Bakr slipped away unnoticed, using unfrequented routes, finally reaching Yathrib in September of 622 AD.

Thus the beginning of the *Hijrah* or Emigration (*A.H./Anno Hegirae*), officially pegged as July 16 of the year 622 AD, marked the starting point of Islamic history.

5. Act (Take Action)

Madinah was in many ways different from the Prophet's original homeland of Makkah. It was an agricultural state which had been developed by the original Arabs, and further enriched by several Jewish clans living there. Later Arab immigrants, the most notable being from the clans of *Al-Aws* and *Al-Khazraj*, were engaged in bitter feuds among themselves, resulting in much bloodshed in a bloody clash at about the year 618 AD.

In welcoming the Prophet Muhammad to Madinah, many of the Arabs there (the people called the *Ansar*) had hoped that he would be able to act as the arbiter and spiritual leader who would rescue them from oppression among the feuding parties, in order to create a just state for all.

The first Constitution of Madinah (*Al-Dustur* or *Al-Watiqah*), was drafted and written, creating a confederation of nine groups, comprising eight Arab clans and the emigrants from Makkah. Although the Prophet did not ask for and was given no special position of authority, the preamble to the constitution referred to the agreement as being formulated between Muhammad the Prophet and the Muslim clans of Madinah, and that all serious disputes were to be arbitrated by him because of the special trust they collectively accorded to him.

In the next five years, the city-state of Madinah took shape as an Islamic bastion. A sense of brotherhood then prevailed, a bond of faith emerged, and Islam acquired its characteristic ethos as a religion of unity governing both the temporal and spiritual aspects of life. There then emerged not only an Islamic religious institution but also an Islamic *Syari'ah* (law-based) state, and related systems governing society at large.

6. Appraise

In Madinah, the Messenger of Allah was received with great enthusiasm by the Muslim quarters of the populace. Anas bin Malik al-Ansari, who was still a boy at the time of the Prophet's eagerly awaited arrival, was reported to have said: "I saw the Messenger of Allah the day he entered Madinah. I have not seen a better or more radiant day than when he came to us in Madinah."

On arrival, the Prophet spent four days at Quba' where he built the first mosque.

Abu Ayyub Al-Ansari hosted the Prophet in his house, showing his guest warm respect and generous hospitality. Abu Ayyub was uneasy staying at the upper level of his house, while his honoured guest placed himself on the lower floor. He feared that he might show disrespect. Prophet Muhammad, however, reassured him saying, "Abu Ayyub, it is more convenient for me and those who call on me that I stay on the lower floor."

The Prophet's mosque in Madinah was built with much sweat and toil. Having bought the piece of land from two orphans, he personally helped construct it, carrying bricks and other building materials alongside his other Muslim brethren. After seven months, the mosque and adjacent rooms for the family quarters were made ready for the Prophet to move into.

The bond of brotherhood and friendship between the emigrant Muhajirun and the native Ansar were reinforced, as each member of the new joint community was under obligation to help one another at all times. A covenant was made with the Jews laying down conditions for their welfare in the new city-state; among the concessions given were the freedom to practise their own religion and their right to keep the titles to their wealth.

The *adzan* (call to prayer) by the *mu'adzin* was instituted. The Messenger of Allah and his Muslim followers prayed facing the *Qiblah* or direction of *Bait al-Maqdis* (Jerusalem) for 16 months in the initial phase of worship. However, the Prophet Muhammad desired to face the Ka'abah, and thus resorted to Allah for wisdom, which was revealed through the verses in Surah *Al-Baqarah*, *2:143-4*. It was thus from then on that Muslims everywhere changed direction when prostrating facing the Ka'abah, the original *qiblah* of his forefathers, the prophets Ibrahim and his son Ismail.

Two significant campaigns (*ghazawah*) were fought at Badr and Uhud, the first won decisively while the second was a reversal with lessons to be learned. The third critical campaign was at Khandaq (battle of the trench), which was one of the most strategically conducted. It was in the year 627 AD when the Makkan leader Abu Sufyan led a massive confederacy of some 10,000 troops against the Muslims in Madinah that ended in misery for the enemy. This time around, the Prophet Muhammad had ordered the agricultural crops around the city-state to be harvested and a long trench to be dug to defend the bastion of Islam in the face of the formidable advancing Makkan cavalry. For two weeks the threatening forces of the confederates laid siege on the Madinan city-state. Yet all attempts to cross the trench failed. Fodder for their horses then became scarce.

The Prophet Muhammad had already planted agents among the enemy forces to foment dissentions. Then finally, after a night swept with fierce winds and rain, the threat of the invading armies fizzled away. They then broke camp and departed.

The Makkans had dispatched their most formidable armed strength but God-willing they failed to dislodge the ardent Muslims, thus considerably strengthening the Prophet of Islam's position in the region.

His farsightedness and wisdom as a military commander and statesman were manifested in the subsequent policies which he adopted and translated into action. He could have chosen to pursue the Makkans and crushed them decisively. But he held back steadfastly, applied economic pressure against them, and more importantly - designed a plan to win them over to Islam. In his wisdom, he knew that in the long run he would need to marshal the entrepreneurial and administrative skills of the Makkan merchants to assist him in propagating Islam in Makkah and along the trade routes to and from Madinah.

Thus the discreet *Treaty of Hudaibiyyah* was covenanted. By early 630 AD, the Prophet Muhammad and his army of 10,000 had marched victoriously, yet unmenacingly, into Makkah, granting amnesty to the general populace, without bloodshed. He was well on the road to unifying the whole of the Arabian Peninsula as a total, holistic Islamic entity!

7. Institutionalise

The question is then duly posed: what legacy has the Prophet Muhammad left behind for posterity? Since the *Hijrah*, he had formed alliances with various clans and tribes, either through non-aggression pacts and covenants, military victories through the many campaigns he conducted, exemplary leadership displayed, as well as marriages arranged in order to build bridges and relationships with the several clans and tribes that existed.

Madinah had begun to take shape as the dominant power in Arabia, and most clans and tribes sent deputations to the city-state, seeking alliances and protection from the egalitarian and democratic centre of influence. The Prophet Muhammad had succeeded to unite most of the Arabian Peninsula, and from there on proceeded to expand the Muslim domain to Syria and Iraq. His major achievements were the strengthening of a religion and statehood. Not only was an Islamic religious establishment securely set up, but an Islamic law, nation and other civilised institutions governing society at large were established. This imprint was replicated in other territories elsewhere in which Islam made its presence felt.

Transformation Management

(Prophet Muhammad's 7-Step Process of Managing Change)

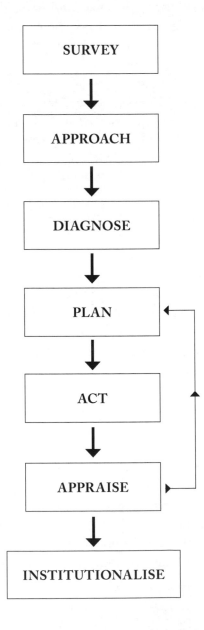

<u>Questions to answer from Chapter 7</u>:

1. Why is transformation/change a critical factor for a leader?

2. Describe briefly what and who is a Visionary Leader.

3. Describe what and who is a Transformational Leader.

4. If transformational leadership involves being first a visionary leader who excites change, describe the comprehensive seven (7) step change process initiated and implemented by the Prophet of Islam.

CHAPTER 8

The Prophet Muhammad as Team Leader

The function of a team is to create high performance through the collective synergy of its members. It has been well proven that soundly-structured teams with efficacious leadership produce admirable results. In the field of sports we have the Real Madrid FC (soccer), the All-Blacks (rugby), the Team Ferrari (Formula 1), and the Ryder Cup Euro (golf) teams. In environmental sustainability we have the Greenpeace; in human rights we have Amnesty International; and in consumerism we have Consumers International. They all function as cohesive teams to achieve astounding sustainable outcomes.

Teams have been around since the beginning of civilizational history: the building of the Great Wall, the charge of the Light Brigade, and the first outer space expedition to the moon – were all outcomes of superior teamwork. No one person could have done it alone, although it is possible of course for one person to create such an impact on others that history is shaped. Thus in the course of human history, we see great leaders with passion and compassion in the persons of movers like the Prophet Muhammad, Jesus, Moses, Buddha, Alexander the Great, Confucius, Columbus, Aristotle, Saladin Ayyub, Napoleon Bonaparte, Nelson Mandela and Mother Teresa. They have, each in their own way, influenced the course of human life and transformed events in history.

The most impacting of all leaders of men is the Prophet Muhammad, who is ranked by the American astrophysicist, historian and author, Michael Hart, as the most influential person in history in his 1992 book, "The 100: A Ranking of the Most Influential Persons in History." He analysed Prophet Muhammad as the most influential, over the prophets Jesus and Moses, attributing it to the fact that the Prophet of Islam was 'supremely successful' in both the religious and secular realms. To be influential is to be convincing; to be convincing is to be able to move masses for purposeful action. The issue of team or collective leadership is significant to the positive development of the Islamic *ummah*, especially when referring to the activities of the *halaqah* (group or circle) or the family unit membership known as the *usrah*.

In the Islamic context, a team comprises at least three people getting together for a common altruistic intent or purpose. The Prophet used to say, *"When travelling on a journey, even if there are only three of you, make one a leader."* Thus when a group of people come together with the objective of doing something worthwhile, they should appoint from among themselves a *qa'id* (Arabic: leader, derived from the Arab word *yaqud* meaning 'he leads'; whereas *qiadah* implies leadership) to provide the guidance and counsel so that the team does not go astray. The leader who is entrusted with the job should be the most competent in the group to handle and see the assignment through, and thus get the mission accomplished according to plan.

In the study of the Prophet of Islam's *Seerah*, team leadership was an important criterion in mission attainment. A team comprises a group of purpose-driven people working together in an extraordinary way, trusting one another, complementing each other's strengths, and compensating for each other's weaknesses. A team embraces collective superordinate goals that are larger than any of the individual goals, and together they consistently produce superior results and outcomes. Effective, high performance teams continuously work together when pursuing their missions, albeit one at a time. A team cannot, therefore, be simply a random get-together of colleagues at work with no specific, planned agenda. It must have a purpose. It must be focused. Members of the team must develop shared values in action.

Such a team is sometimes called **tanzim haraki**. The term *tanzim* refers to an organized, structured, disciplined, coordinated, and interpersonally connected team of people who collectively set out to achieve a common, predetermined goal under the leadership of the *qa'id*, who is responsible for managing their well-being while striving to realise their mutually-shared objectives. In doing so, the members who are regulated by the *tanzim* are collectively bound by a code of conduct and set of rules or regulations that define their rights and regulations to get the job done. It is obligatory on the part of both the leader and followers to abide by the agreed-upon code and specific guidelines.

The word *haraki* implies a movement of people in joint action, moving forward assertively and positively. In modern times, we often hear of the *saemaul undong* movement in South Korea, which evokes eulogies in the spirit of community development among the country's people at all levels emanating from the Malaysian *gotong royong* community self-help concept. In Japan, we have other countries emulating the renowned Japanese bottom-up *nemawashi* process of group problem-solving and decision-making, and even in South Africa, the government had embarked (since the time Nelson Mandela became president) on a synergistic campaign they call *Masakhane* (in Nguni it means: "Let us build together!"), conveying the spirit of the people to create a concerted movement to build a united nation, thus evoking a deep sense of community, belonging and pride - after many years of tormented apartheid rule.

Every single member of a team is responsible and accountable for the due performance of the tasks at hand so that collectively they are able to synergize and focus their minds on accomplishing the mission. It is important for each member to understand that 'a chain is only as strong as its weakest link." In order for the team to be effective, a SWOT (Strengths, Weaknesses, Opportunities, and Threats) analysis has to be done to assess the team's individual and collective competencies. What needs to be avoided is the emergence of one-too-many 'champions' who may be strong individually but perform miserably as a team. Such so-called champions need to be moulded into 'team players,' either by positive conditioning, orientation or structured training.

It should be a fact of life that any sound, able and capable person can perform the role of a *qa'id* or leader. One can perform this role either *de jure* (one who has the legal right to lead, with the authority entrusted upon him to do so) in form, or *de facto* (one who is unofficially or situationally positioned to lead) in practice.

A team should have an identity to stand up to and be recognised. Identity refers to a state of being certain about oneself regarding purpose, philosophy, character, and reason for existence (*raison d'etre*). The team's identity reflects its distinguishing character and is often emblazoned with a coat-of-arms, the inscription of a logo, the unfurling of a flag, the displaying of a banner, or the wearing of a badge on the uniform. Often times, a chant or war cry (like the New Zealand All Blacks rugby team's *hakka*) is chanted to echo the team's clarion call for victory. A team that is devoid of a recognisable identity is said to be saddled with an identity crisis. In the Battle of Badr, and in subsequent *ghazawah* (campaigns), the Prophet of Islam held his own banner to lead his warriors into the believers' first battle against the enemy.

The Prophet of Islam had carefully chosen the membership of his *Tanzim Haraki Islami* from the ranks of those who subscribed to the Oneness of Allah Almighty, with Islam as the religion of choice, and Muhammad as the final Messenger. Out of these he designated the leaders, who then assumed the roles of military commanders, governors, judges, emissaries, tax collectors, administrators, and others.

Archimedes, the foremost mathematician and inventor in ancient Greece in the 3rd Century BC, once said: *"Give me a lever long enough…and single-handed I can move the world."*

The Prophet Muhammad had the holy Qur'an as the lever to greatness, and with the sanctity of revealed knowledge, he played the role of **designer team leader**. As the designer leader, he managed to create such a profound and sweeping influence. Over the relatively short duration of 23 years since prophethood, he inspired and grand-designed an empire sprawling territorially from North Africa into Spain, Syria, Iran, India, Southeast Asia and into Far Eastern China – an empire that was rich in culture, theology, philosophy, science, administration, and commerce. Throughout history, leaders who play the designer role do not consciously seek to hog the limelight. They prefer to work quietly, conscientiously, and dedicatedly to achieve their superordinate vision of greatness. Those who practise this style of leadership truly find deep satisfaction in empowering others who in turn feel superbly motivated being part of an organization producing the kind of outcomes they could really proud of.

In today's *realpolitik* world, the leader as designer role is unfortunately much neglected. Most so-called team leaders, be they at unit, departmental, organizational, national, international or even global levels, easily fall prey to their *shahwah* (base desires) and crave for fame, control, hegemony, and self-centredness on the pretext of being action-oriented saviours of humankind.

The ancient Chinese philosopher of around 500 BC, Lao-tze, was quoted as having said, *"A bad leader is he who the people despise. The good leader is he who the people praise. The great leader is he who the people (followers) say: he made it look as if we did it ourselves!"* Such is the magnanimous challenge facing anyone who aspires to lead a team to greatness.

Transformation of Arab society

When the Prophet Muhammad emigrated with his loyal companion, Abu Bakr as-Sadiq, (and subsequently followed by his band of devoted followers), to Yathrib (later renamed Madinah) in 622 AD, he proposed to the believers that the new Islamic city-state should assume a political character. The suggestion was openly received by both the emigrant Muhajirun and the host Ansar population. The political structure proposed by the Prophet would prevent the continuance of internal strife and bloodshed among the contentious, confrontational tribes and factions – at the time a common feature of what society was like in Yathrib.

The proposal would also strengthen the city state's proneness to possible external threats and attacks. After articulating his proposal, the Prophet concretised his plan into the framework of the first written *Al-Dustur* (State Constitution). All citizens of the populace, comprising the two main tribes of the Ansar community, the Jewish factions, the Christians, and the Bedouin pagans were brought into the mainstream of life.

Among the landmark features the Prophet of Islam initiated were:

- **Abolishment of slavery and class distinction**

  For a start, the Prophet Muhammad had enfranchised his slave, Zaid ibn Harithah. By this action alone, it conveyed the message to society that slavery was not to be tolerated.

Within the city-state of Madinah, there was to be no distinction between the ruler and the ruled. There was to be no barriers of class, colour, or descent. The Prophet had decreed, *"The noblest in the sight of God Almighty is the one who is most virtuous among men."*

Madinah was fast becoming a dynamic hub of activity embracing the Islamic *syari'ah*. Prophet Muhammad was revered not only as the Messenger of Allah, but also as the political and administrative leader of the newly-structured city-state. The newly established Islamic state was a to be a haven for all, male or female, and everyone subscribed and belonged to One God Almighty, subject to His revealed laws.

The master-slave relationship, as traditionally practised, was condemned. He made a covenant with the traditionally hostile Jewish population, granting them the freedom to practise their religion and allowing them to keep their property and wealth (except that they had to pay tax or *jizyah* to protect their security and interests). Islam began to take root in Madinah, and some rabbis and Jewish scholars were so enraptured by the Prophet's just and equitable policies that they even became Muslims.

- **Injunctions to prayer, *zakat*, fasting and quality of life**

With the establishment of the political and administrative entity came several authoritative divine injunctions from God Almighty for the holistic well-being of the community. The call for daily prayers (*adzan*), facing the direction of the Ka'abah, was adhered to. Other dutiful obligations which the believers must fulfil include the observance of fasting (*siam*), to attain wellness of mind, body and soul. The payment of tithe (*zakat*) was offered by those who could afford as a welfare-due to seek purification of one's earnings entitling Allah's blessings:

"The likeness of those who expend their wealth in the way of Allah is as like a seed (of grain or corn) that sprouts seven ears, in every ear a hundred grains. So Allah multiplies (His reward) for whom He wills. Allah is All-Embracing, All-Knowing".

[Qur'an, Al-Baqarah, The Cow, 2:261]

Wine and gambling, which used to dominate life in Madinah and which caused disorderly and riotous scenes, were now prohibited:

"O you who believe; liquor and gambling, idols and raffles, are only some filthy work of Satan; avoid them so that you may prosper. Satan only wants to stir up enmity and jealousy among you by means of liquor and gambling, and to hinder you from praying. So will you refrain?"

[Qur'an, Al-Ma'idah, The Food, 5:90-91]

The Prophet and his core team of followers not only spent time formalising the ritualistic aspects of Islam. Verses were judiciously revealed for the guidance of the believers: and matters pertaining to economic activities, social codes of behaviour, and parameters were established for their socio-political well-being and development.

• **Brotherhood pact (*Mu'akhah*)**

The Messenger of Allah took great pains to forge inter-communal unity by establishing a pact of brotherhood between the emigrant Muhajirun and the host Ansar. They were each obliged to help one another at all times. In fact, the Ansar were so eager to form the brotherhood that they had to queue up to allocate their shares to their emigrant brothers. The Ansar gave the Muhajirun authority over their homes, furniture, land, and animal stock and preferred their brethren over themselves. This selfless, altruistic gesture truly emulated the Prophet's own way of living.

An Ansar would say to a Muhajirun, "Please have whichever half of my property you want," and the Muhajir would respond, "May Allah bless you and your family and property! But show me the market and we will maintain ourselves by working for our living." The Muhajirun, being traditionally traders, had to adjust themselves to the new agricultural environment of their counterparts in order to co-exist. The Prophet exhorted them, *"Fraternise in the cause of Allah, for you are brothers!"*

In the context of modern management, it could be said that the system of *mu'akhah* is somewhat akin to what is today known as 'mentoring'. In a generic sense, mentoring entails coaching, counseling, and role-modeling. The Prophet Muhammad was the ideal mentor to imbibe the wisdom and skills of mentoring. The aim was to foster closeness in relationships through the process of coaching, or showing how the Ansar could transfer the skills of agricultural practices to their Muhajirun brothers, and in return the latter could show how to market and trade their produce at the marketplace. Counseling was by way of giving mutually appropriate advice when problems arose while conducting such activities. Overseeing these was the role-modeling stance of the Prophet.

Team Building – Creating the Right Balance

Prophet Muhammad formulated the concept of team balance in getting the best out of his Companions. As the Prophet of Allah, he was acknowledged as the *de jure* leader, but he recognised that his Companions could well play their supplementary role as *de facto* leaders since he had taken pains to analyse the individual strengths of each one of them. He enabled them to contribute to the collective leadership role as and when the specific occasion demanded. He was always ready to acknowledge their contributions by way of the skills and expertise they could render, while recognising the individual personalities that each displayed.

The Prophet Muhammad is acknowledged as an exemplary team leader who knew how to get the best out of his principal lieutenants by understanding the true value of the human capital factor. Among his principal lieutenants were leaders of varied styles, personalities and competencies. By being constantly mindful of their differing qualities and strengths, he was able to galvanise their efforts towards the attainment of shared superordinate goals. The ability to forge a cohesive and results-oriented team, with a deep sense of mission, is best achieved when one is able to exercise *team balance* to attain predetermined outcomes.

Effective teamwork stems from people complementing, rather than rivaling each other or merely co-existing alongside one another. It involves understanding the common key objectives, creating a shared sense of mission or purpose, being constantly alert, and judiciously braving the odds.

The governance of the city-state of Madinah was in the hands of the Majlis Shura or the Consultative Council, the leading members of Prophet Muhammad's team being:

1. Abu Bakr As-Sadiq
2. Umar Al-Khattab
3. Uthman Al-Affan
4. Ali ibn Abi Talib
5. Zaid ibn Thabit Al-Ansari
6. Abdul Rahman bin 'Awf
7. Salman Al-Farsi
8. 'Ubayy bin Ka'b

The composition of the Prophet's lead team (the *Majlis Shura*) warrants an analysis of the balance between personality traits and functions. Personality traits contribute to the role each member plays while functions relate to the designation each member is entrusted with.

Prophet Muhammad clearly insisted upon the often fleeting quality of integrity among those who were selected to be leaders of the *ummah*, the ever-expanding Muslim community. For the Prophet of Islam, there was no avenue for any element of bribery, corruption or dishonesty. This prohibition might seem to be a tall order then, for the Qur'an warns that man is 'violent...in the love of wealth.'

[Qur'an, Al-Adiyat, The Assaulters, 100:8].

The Prophet Muhammad himself had given his tacit assurance to his followers who promise to abide by a code of ethics. "I will stand surety for Paradise if you save yourself from six (sinful) things":

- telling untruths
- violating promises
- dishonouring trust
- being unchaste in thought and action
- striking the first blow, and
- taking what is bad and unlawful."

His moral intelligence showed that he was the most competent to ensure that the development of the city-state of Madinah would be in the hands of a team of Companions who would strive along the straight path of good governance and work towards the *jihadic* goal of universal felicity through synergy.

Team Balance Profile in the Prophet's Consultative Council Membership
(*Majlis Shura*)

Name	Personality Traits (Strength, Character and Disposition)	Designation
Abu Bakr	Cool, composed, self-possessed – with robust common sense. The Prophet's closest and most trustworthy friend.	Prophet's Confidante First Caliph
Umar	Strong-willed, explosive, short-tempered yet sentimental. Had immense common sense. Just and disciplined. Remarkable capacity to own up his rash decisions.	Prophet's Yeoman. Second Caliph
Uthman	Unassuming, retiring, forgiving, fore-bearing, and large-hearted. Wealthy businessman of the Umayyad clan of Quraish. High in esteem. Principled. Generously donated to the cause.	Prophet's personal envoy to Makkah. Third Caliph
Ali	Man of letters. Gentlemanly. Lots of courage. Independent-minded. Very close to the Prophet's family.	Scholar. Fourth Caliph. Moved capital to Kufah
Zaid	Intelligent. Has the ability to read and write. Learned and competent. Recorded the Qur'an.	The Prophet's official scribe.
Abd Rahman	Good physique and features. Stood by the Prophet through thick and thin. He is trusted and respected by all. Of very high integrity. Severely wounded at the Battle of Uhud.	One of Umar's trusted lieutenants. Presided Committee of Six.

| Salman | Persian-born, originally a Christian. Bought and freed from slavery by the Prophet. Sincere. Paragon of piety, wisdom, and learning. Denizen of the House of the Prophet (*Ahl-ul-Bait*). | Made Governor of Kufah by Caliph Umar |
| 'Ubayy | Regarded as front-ranked jurist in the early days of Islam. | Scribe for the recording of the Qur'an. |

The mode of team leadership executed by the Prophet of Islam can cross-comparatively be analysed against the mnemonic acronym BEST, elucidated by a current authority in this field, Dr Meredith Belbin.

- **B**alancing the Team
  The leader must ensure that the team is either judiciously balanced, or that imbalances are well noted and compensated for. In the Prophet's Consultative Council (*Majlis Shura*), the team composition was well-balanced in terms of personalities and functions. Each one of them executed a specific function and played a definitive role.

- **E**xploiting the Diversity
  The members of the team are different, requiring different strokes for different folks. It becomes the key task of the leader to ensure that everyone is made to contribute (nobody should be regarded as dysfunctional) and that all the diverse skills and traits are brought to bear upon the results. The Prophet knew how to utilise the diverse strengths of each one of his team members, thus creating also an effective leadership succession framework.

- **S**haring the Goal
  The leader must ensure that everyone understands and agrees exactly what it is that the team is trying to achieve together. This involves giving mutual feedback so that team members truly understand where they are and whether they have arrived in terms of attaining the goal. For every major campaign, the Prophet ensured that each key member of his team knew in advance what was in store in terms of strategy, objectives and attainment standards.

- <u>T</u>rusting the Team
  The leader cannot and must not do it all alone, for as the saying goes, "no man is an island." Indeed the leader's most important consideration should be on how to make the team work together synergistically. The leader must trust the team members and act as a mentor to get on with the job at hand and allow them the requisite freedom that they need to get the mission well executed. The Prophet assigned specific responsibilities and roles to each of his Companions. They thus put their minds and hearts to the task at hand, in the cause of Allah Almighty.

The acronym BEST is a pragmatic way to being held accountable for attaining the desired outcome.

Being held accountable

Accountability is a vital concept in managerial leadership. It establishes that leaders are held answerable for the stewardship and well-being of everything that is carried out under their jurisdiction. In individual accountability, one cannot run away from being answerable for the desired outcomes. In order to ensure that all outcomes are desired ones, the managerial leader has to formulate at the outset a specific mission statement for every purposeful assignment that is to be executed by the team. This calls for clear accompanying objectives and targets, effective monitoring and control procedures, and prompt and meaningful rewards for performance accomplishments. Accountability clarifies and empowers the tasks of managers and those they lead.

It begins with the leader proclaiming, "If it's got to be, let it be me!" No scapegoating, no apportioning of blame, no finger-pointing if things do not go right at the end of the day.

"Every person is accountable for what he earns, for no bearer of a burden bears the burden of another."

[Qur'an, Al-An'am, The Cattle, 6:164]

Everyone who is placed in a leadership function is responsible and accountable for his own entrusted performance attainment level and that on no account can this be shifted from one to another. The Prophet stated:

"I am accountable for my actions and you are for yours: you are not accountable for what I do. Everyone of you is a shepherd and everyone is responsible for what he is shepherd of."

[Sahih Bukhari and Muslim]

Whilst responsibility can be delegated, accountability cannot. In Islam, accountability is a personal mandate to deliver. The Prophet was entrusted with the task of providing dual leadership, i.e. the efficacious (doing things right, while doing the right things) spiritual and political guidance of the world according to divine commandment and the *syari'ah*. He was the Messenger and mentor, as well as serving as commander, judge and proselytiser. He moulded a nation from scratch to reach the pinnacle of spiritual and moral excellence, and over a relatively short span of 23 years, attained political supremacy over all other powers in the region. He never blamed anyone for any temporary shortcomings that might have arisen.

The Qur'an forewarns:

"Whoever adopts the righteous way, his righteous conduct will be for his own good, and whoever goes astray, his deviation shall bring its consequences on him. Nor bearer of a burden will bear the burden of another."

[Qur'an, Al-Israa', The Israelites, 17:15]

The principle of moral accountability is all-encompassing in Islamic management. It embraces both the temporal and spiritual aspects and applies to the individual actions of a Muslim as well as his actions in the service of his community.

Accountability is applicable to both tasks and results. The performance attainment model emphasizing management by objectives (MBOs) and key performance indices (KPIs) need to be adjusted to achieve a balanced scorecard (BSC) that seriously takes into consideration the human factor. The Muslim leader has to be continually mindful of his relationships with his Creator as well as his people (*Hablum-min-Allah, wa hablum-min-an-nas*). In gunning for results, he has to do so in a manner that does not deviate from the *Syari'ah*, nor offend, condescend, or patronise his people. He should not be high-nosed about things nor unduly brash when addressing or reprimanding others. The emphasis on how the work is done and what results are attained is important because they avoid prejudging people by their character traits alone.

The leader should also specify the desired standards of performance so that followers are clear at the outset about what are expected of them in each of their designated assignments. As results are usually the consequence of work processes, it makes good sense to monitor the work done from start to finish to ascertain the team is on track.

Just as accountability cannot be delegated, it cannot compulsively be shared. This is because we cannot effectively hold groups (remember *groupthink*?) accountable for results and outcomes. The leader designated to the task at hand must bear the consequence of any misfortune.

As a case in point, during the military campaign at Uhud, the Prophet had clearly issued specific instructions to his designated force of archers not to leave their strategically guarded position at the gap up the hill under any circumstance. But on seeing the enemy losing ground lower down the hill, they left their outpost and swooped downhill upon the fleeing enemy with greed (for the booty), thus leaving the gap to be occupied and secured by enemy reinforcements which attacked them from behind.

The undesired consequence? The Muslim forces suffered a reversal that could have cost the life of the Prophet himself. It was a painful lesson which the Muslims learnt early in the history of their statehood – not to disobey the Prophet, an object lesson in followership God Almighty had ordained never to be repeated. The implication is that whatever the Prophet of Allah commands it should be obeyed, and whatever he forbids should be refrained from.

"O you who believe! Obey Allah and His Messenger, and turn not away from him while you are hearing."
                                    [Qur'an, Al-Anfal, The Spoils of War, 8:20]

The principle of personal responsibility and accountability in modern times can be extended to individual organizations, institutions, corporations, nations – even at international or global levels. Those privileged to head such public organizations (Directors-General), corporations (CEOs), institutions (secretaries-general), and nations (prime ministers/presidents) are held accountable for the due performance of their charges.

The Qur'an cautions leaders:

"They were a nation who has passed away. They shall receive the reward of what they earned and you shall have the reward of what you earn; and you will not be questioned as to what they did."

[Qur'an, Al-Baqarah, The Cow, 2:134 & 141]

This verse is an emphatic outreach to leaders of organizations and nation-states to be conscious and mindful of their roles in keeping the peace, security and well-being of their peoples intact. It cautions that individuals elected to high office must be held accountable for their own actions and outcomes. Japanese leadership seems to embrace this concept better, that when something really undesirable occurs, the head himself offers to let go of his position.

"Ten soldiers wisely led, will beat a hundred without a head."

[Euripides]

In recent times, many a prime minister and corporate chieftains have come and gone. Those who made it subscribe to no scapegoating, no blameworthiness, no finger-pointing. As Konosuke Matsushita, founder president of Matsushita Electric Industrial Co., and at one time the foremost leader in Japanese industry said,

"A company's president is solely and personally responsible for his firm's success or failure, and he must not try to pass the buck."

It has been a central feature of modern management that when a disaster occurs within the jurisdiction of a Japanese organization, it is the topmost personnel who takes the rap. There is no attempt to pass the buck downwards. The most senior man resigns.

In one critical incident after the news of the Muslim army's victory in the conquest of Syria, the second Caliph Umar had advanced to Damascus with a number of his Companions. On reaching the outskirts of 'Amwas, a Syrian town, the news of a widespread outbreak of a plague in the town reached him. Umar engaged in mutual consultation with his Companions as to whether they should continue to venture forth into the town. The intense deliberations that followed came to a conclusion when Abdul Rahman ibn 'Awf cited a saying of the Prophet,

"If you are inside a place where an epidemic breaks out, don't come out of it. And don't go in if you happen to be away from such a place."

Taking stock of what the Prophet had stated, Umar commanded his troops to withdraw from the periphery of the town. Somebody had then hastened to remark on Umar's apparent retreat, "Umar, do you run away from a destiny decreed by Allah?" To which Umar retorted, "Yes, we run away from one destiny to the other decreed by Allah as well."

Such was the prevailing wisdom of the Prophet which, even as far back as several double-digit decades ago, had foreshadowed today's strict quarantine regulations. Caliph Umar saw his role as the arbiter of the Prophet's decree, and acted on it by the principle of personal accountability, to protect the environment from a widespread health hazard.

Accountability is certainly not an abstract concept. It is meaningfully pivotal to the effective practice of managerial, political and spiritual leadership. The *sunnah* of the Prophet provides substantial instances and examples of its efficacy.

Questions to answer from Chapter 8

1. Define what a team is. Why is team identity important?

2. What do you understand by the term *Tanzim Haraki?*

3. Explain three of the landmark features initiated by the Prophet in Madinah.

4. Discuss the importance of team balance in the Prophet's Consultative Council (*Majlis Shura*).

5. What do you understand by the concept of accountability?

6. Why is personal accountability important in team efficacy?

CHAPTER 9

Prophet Muhammad - the Family Man

The versatility of a supreme leader who excels in all areas of his life needs to be justly told and shared, in order to be emulated. In real life, Muhammad is the only person in history whose life example can serve as a model for all mankind.

"Indeed, in the Messenger of Allah (Muhammad), you have an excellent example to follow for him who hopes for (the Meeting with) Allah and the Last Day, and remembers Allah much."

[Qur'an, Al-Ahzab, The Allies, 33:21]

Prophet Muhammad was perfect in every sense of the word, living a most exemplary life; and yet like any human being in a high position of leadership he had to create a good balance among the following factors that he had to address:

- experiencing the joys and sorrows of family existence
- executing bargaining and negotiating strategies as a businessman
- grappling with the challenges and hardships of war as a military commander
- making judicious decisions as a judge, arbiter and mediator
- contending with evil and corruptive forces as a revered rector
- conscientiously striving to establish a civilised new world order

such that it was amazing how he could allocate the time attending to all these requirements and attention-needers.

The family life of a leader is the real mirror of his personal nature, behaviour and character. The best test of his quality as a person and leader is at his own home. For instance, how much does he himself practise the critical belief in the fear of Allah (*Taqwa*) and the compassion which he preaches to other people? How much does he himself observe the Holy Qur'an and the *Sunnah* that he is exhorting others to follow? How far does his own family abide by and practise those same principles and concepts that he preaches to the outside world? How much of the teaching of moderation: simple living, sacrifice, patience, contentment, honesty, good ethics and moral values that he is demanding of others are visible in his own home? If the leader comes out successful in this test, he would have proven his high moral values, virtuous character, and upright truthfulness.

With this backdrop in mind, compare the life tapestry of the Prophet Muhammad himself in the context of this test. His life history has been well recorded in the *Seerah* and *hadith*, which are based on authentic reports and records of what he said and did especially among the ranks of his Companions. So transparent are the observations that we even know today what he did and how he spent his time with members of his immediate and extended families. Both his private and public life are like an open book to all and sundry, and this gives people of all shades and walks of life the opportunity to understand and emulate him, regardless of their backgrounds. Whatever noble work he himself partook in, his family members also did the same.

"It is He Who has sent amongst the unlettered a Messenger from among themselves, to recite to them His verses, to purify them (from disbelief and polytheism), and to instruct them in the Book (the Qur'an, Islamic laws and jurisprudence) and Al-Hikmah (Wisdom of the As-Sunnah: legal ways, orders, acts of worship of Prophet Muhammad)."
[Qur'an, Al-Jumu'ah, Friday, 62:2]

In Islam, the basic unit of human society is the family, moulded through the legal marriage of man and woman. According to the Qur'an, a marriage should not just be based on the considerations of beauty, wealth or family connections, but greatly on moral or spiritual considerations. The Prophet Muhammad took pains to emphasize these principles of marriage when he used to attend or preside over marriage occasions.

The Prophet Muhammad also stressed that women have rights in relation to their menfolk, on the basis of justice and equity. Men are exhorted to live with their wives in kindness. He never missed to point out: "The best among you is he who treats the members of his family best."

What Prophet Muhammad set out to establish in Makkan society was in stark contrast with what was then the norm. "In old Arabia, the husband was so indifferent to his wife's fidelity, that he might send her to cohabit with another man to get himself a goodly seed."

[W. Robertson Smith, *Kinship and Marriage in Early Arabia, 2nd Edition,
London, 1903, p.116*].

There was no element of illegitimacy attached to the child of a harlot. Polyandry, by which a woman takes more than one man as her husband was very common in paganistic Arabia; and there was no distinction between legitimate and illegitimate offsprings in the civilised sense of the word. Prophet Muhammad was about to change all that.

Prophet Muhammad as a husband

The necessity for marriage is spelt out in the *Shari'ah* and in custom as the Prophet's *sunnah*. For the leader, it is a proof of perfection and sound masculinity. The Prophet had pointed out, "Whoever has the capacity should marry. It lowers the eyes and protects the private parts."

[Hadith At-Tabarani, and Muslim and Al-Bukhari].

A person who is able to marry and carry out the obligations that come along with it without being distracted from the remembrance of his Lord has a lofty degree. Such is the degree of the Prophet Muhammad.

Having several wives did not distract him from consistently worshipping his Lord. On the contrary, it enhanced his standing as a devoted worshipper in that he dutifully protected his wives, gave them their rights, earned for them, and truly guided them along the straight path in the cause of Allah Almighty.

Prophet Muhammad's wives, by choice, were specially selected by Allah to help him in the pursuit and completion of his mission on earth. They were asked to play the role of 'mothers' of all Muslim men and women such that people can take them as models emulating what the holy Prophet did and taught.

"O wives of the Prophet! You are not like any other women. If you keep your duty (to Allah), then be not soft in speech (to men), lest he in whose heart is a disease (of hypocrisy, or evil desire for adultery) should be moved with desire, but speak in an honourable manner. And stay in your houses, and do not display yourselves like that of the times of ignorance, and perform As-Salat, and give zakat and obey Allah and His Messenger. Allah only wishes to remove Ar-Rijs (evil deeds and sins) from you, O members of the family (of the Prophet), and to purify you with a thorough purification. And remember (the graces of your Lord) that which is recited in your houses of the Verses of Allah and Al-Hikmah (i.e. Prophet's Sunnah – legal ways, so give your thanks to Allah and glorify His Praises for this Qur'an and the Sunnah). Verily, Allah is Ever Most Courteous, Well-Acquainted (with all things)."

[Qur'an, Al-Ahzab, The Allies, 33:32-34]

His family life was full of joys, sorrows and challenges, like most other decent family's. And just because the Prophet and his household chose poverty instead of abundance, service in the cause of humanity rather than service of self, the Hereafter instead of just this temporal world - it did not mean that there was no merriment or varied activities in his overall family life.

Truly, as a responsible husband, he was very affectionate and loving to all his wives. He trusted his wives greatly and shared some of his most intimate secrets with them. However, if there was any weakness on the part of his wives in keeping secrets, he would judiciously reprimand them. Sometimes, he would engage in humourous banter and fun with them.

It was one day when one of his wives asked him who among them was his most favourite loving wife. He would respond to her by saying that it was the one whom he gave a ring as a present. So he gave the wife who asked a ring. But he cautioned her to keep it a secret and not to tell the other wives. Coincidentally, it so happened that over time, each and every one of his wives had asked him the same question, and he gave each the same answer: "the wife I love most is the one I'm giving this ring to…so here is the ring that I'm giving you, but make sure that you do not tell any of my other wives about this!" Because everyone was given a ring in a separate house (they were not all staying under one roof) and on a separate occasion, they were each thinking, "Ah, I'm the one he loves most of all," and thus they were all individually happy at the same time!

It is true that as a husband, he had a unique relationship with his first wife, Khadijah, as his subsequent marriages after her death were based on a number of considerations prevailing at the time. In spite of the difference in age, his love for Khadijah never once wavered. When death parted her from the Prophet in 618 AD, he deeply mourned her death, especially when reminiscing what they had shared together through the many arduous years of trials and tribulations, notably in the first few years of his propagating Islam in Makkah. Once A'ishah asked the Prophet if she had been the only woman worthy of his love, he replied with the most sincere showing of tender emotion:

"She believed in me when no one else did, she embraced Islam when people disbelieved me, and she helped and comforted me when there was none to lend a helping hand."

As an ideal husband, Prophet Muhammad had set a good example of married life and displayed how the relationship between a husband and wife should be conducted, based on the injunctions of the Qur'an, on the basis of the tenderest form of devotion on both sides and by mutual love and affection. The Qur'an, and hence Islam, lays down guidelines about husband-and-wife relationship and the Prophet Muhammad was the noblest exemplar of that ideal relationship.

The lover of children

The Prophet Muhammad was especially fond of children. He was considerate, gentle and affectionate towards them. Sadly, the Prophet lost all his sons when they were infants. He adopted a slave-boy, Zaid, son of Harithah, as his son for whom he had genuine love and affection too. He cultivated close friendships with all his children and grandchildren, playing and cheerfully joking with them to make them happy. He was very fond of the sons of his daughter, Fatimah, Hasan and Hussain; and one of his grand-daughters, Ummah, was also a favourite child. He would be heard saying, "God I love them, love them thus."

In Islam, each child is regarded as a trust from God Almighty, and all his/her physical and mental capacities and powers are gifts from Him. No stone should be left unturned and uncared for in terms of providing the necessary facilities for the full growth and development of the character and personality of the child. The whole Islamic system and its many organs should always be galvanised to ensure that each child is developed in the right pathway of Islam. During the period of *Jahiliyyah*, before Prophet Muhammad's time, children and especially girls, were badly treated and abused.

The Prophet Muhammad abolished (child) female infanticide, a customary practice during the period of ignorance, during which female daughters were killed by parents to offset the mistaken belief that poverty would befall them if they were allowed to live. When he conquered Makkah, the Prophet Muhammad formally demanded a promise from Arab society not to commit child murder.

Prophet Muhammad's childhood is a reflection of his care and compassion for children and others under his stewardship. He himself was hardly six years old when his mother died, and the charge of his childhood fell on his grandfather, Abd al-Muttalib, who doted his grandchild. But two years later, his aged grandfather passed away, and Muhammad was again in sorrow. The charge of Muhammad then fell into the arms of his uncle (his father's brother), Abu Talib. Like all other young boys of his age, the young Muhammad tended to the sheep and goats of farm owners in Makkah, grazing them on the surrounding hills and valleys.

As a prophet in the making, the vocation of attending to the flocks as a junior youth is congenial to the thoughtful and meditative temperament. "While he watched the flocks, his attention would be riveted by the signs of the Unseen Power gliding through the dark blue sky silently along, and these would be charged to him with a special message..."

By way of analogy, the tending of flocks of sheep and goats became the preparatory ground for the training of humankind. The shepherd is always on the alert when taking care of his flock so that they do not graze unlawfully into somebody's farm or fold, or render them easy prey to predators or wild beasts.

In a metaphorical sense, from time immemorial, the best comparison for a leader is that of the shepherd. The shepherd gives direction to his flock by leading it from the front, at times having to trek up to 20 miles a day, in search of available grass growing in the far distance. When a shepherd walks behind the flock, it is because he has to be mindful of the stragglers as well as to protect them from unwelcome predators like wolves or hyenas. The shepherd has at times to walk alongside the flock, somewhere at the middle to keep the sheep or goats in line. For large flocks the shepherd may be assisted by the under-shepherd or helper who can help bring up the rear. The ability to keep the flock close together is important to ensure its safety and wellbeing.

Such is also the case for the future prophet of Allah. The Prophet Muhammad was reported to have said, "*There is no prophet that has not worked as a shepherd.*" Prophets David, Jacob and Jesus spent time as shepherds. Each prophet served as the shepherd to humankind; always mindful of their wellbeing and progress along the straight path. It was from this valuable experience as a shepherd that later sprang up the love for the humankind, beginning with the family and children.

For Muslims, part of the respect and devotion to the Prophet Muhammad, is the devotion to his immediate family, his wives and descendants. Zayd ibn Arqam related that the Messenger of Allah said, "*I implore you by Allah! The people of my house!*" repeating the supplication three times. When asked, Zayd clarified that those who constituted the Prophet's 'people of the house' were the family of 'Ali (the Prophet's cousin/son-in-law), the family of Ja'far (a son of Abu Talib), the family of 'Uqay (another son of Abu Talib), and the family of Al-'Abbas (his uncle).

The Prophet also said, "I am leaving you something, taking hold of which will prevent you from going astray: the Book of Allah and my family, the people of my house. So take care how you follow me regarding them."

[Rawahu Tirmidhi]

Questions to answer from Chapter 9:

1. Why should a leader be judged by his ability to manage his family?

2. Describe the Prophet Muhammad as an ideal husband and family man.

3. Describe the Prophet Muhammad as a lover of children.

4. Why is the *shepherd* a good metaphorical comparison to family stewardship?

CHAPTER 10

Pen Picture of the Prophet Muhammad

A'ishah, Prophet Muhammad's devoted wife, testified that her husband's character and conduct personified the teachings of the Qur'an. Whatever the Qur'an exhorts and commands, the Prophet followed it to the letter. The Holy Book of Allah itself states that the Prophet's character is the most exemplary for all of mankind.

The Prophet Muhammad was born in 570 AD, but was orphaned by the age of 6. He was then brought up by his grandfather, Abdul-Muttalib and then by his uncle, Abu Talib, who protected him from the torment imposed by the Quraish chiefs of the time in Makkah.

In his youth, he worked as a shepherd and later as a caravan leader. When his age reached 24, he worked as a trading caravan leader for a wealthy noble widow named Khadijah, who eventually became his devoted, loving wife.

In the year 610 AD, while sojourning in a cave on Mount Hira' wrapped in his cloak, he was approached by the arch-angel Gabriel and given the first divine revelation:

"Read! In the Name of your Lord Who has created (all that exists). Created man from a clinging substance. Read, and your Lord is the most Generous. Who taught by the pen. Taught man that which he knew not."

[Qur'an, Al-Alaq, The Clot, 96:1-5]

Although Muhammad was unlettered, he was coached by Gabriel to read. The significance of this is that Muslims wherever they are, are all obliged to read and gain knowledge in life, especially from the holy Qur'an.

For the next dozen years he propagated the new faith, at first secretly, and then openly through trials and tribulations. When Khadijah and Abu Talib passed away in *circa* 618 AD, and when his personal safety in Makkah was endangered, Prophet Muhammad accepted the invitation of the Ansar (helpers/allies) to emigrate to Yathrib (later renamed Madinah). This journey is known as the *Hijrah*, which means dissociation or migration.

Ali ibn Abi Talib, who was the cousin and later son-in-law of the Prophet Muhammad, was the closest kin and had the following to say of the Messenger of Allah:

"He was not coarse or obscene and he did not shout in the market-place. He did not return evil for evil, but was glad to forgive and forget. He did not lay his hands on anyone save in jihad and he did not strike anybody, neither a servant nor a woman. I never saw him take revenge for any offence so long as it was not violating the honour of Allah. When a limitation set by Allah was violated, however, he would be more enraged than anyone else. Given a choice between two courses, he would always choose the simpler of the two."

When he entered his house, he behaved like other ordinary men; he cleaned his own garments, milked his goat, and carried out household chores.

He never stood up or sat down without the name of Allah being mentioned on his lips. Wherever he went, he would sit by the side or the back of the gathering, not wanting to be conspicuous. He gave all those who sat with him such attention that they believed he had paid more heed to them than to anyone else. When someone sat with him, he was attentive and patient throughout until it was time for that person to depart. When someone asked him for help, he would either give him what he needed or speak words of kindness to him.

He was always positive and tender-hearted. He treated everyone as equals. He was the most generous of people, the most truthful, the kindest and the noblest. Those meeting him for the first time were overawed, but those who knew him well loved him."

Allah has endowed His Prophet with elegance and grace, and bestowed upon him love and dignity.

Companion Al-Bara' ibn 'Azib described him, saying:

"The Messenger of Allah was of medium height. I saw him wearing a red-striped robe and I have never seen anything more beautiful than he."

Another close Companion, Abu Hurairah described him, saying:

"He was on the tall side of medium, with very fair skin. His hair was black, and he had excellent front teeth. His eyelashes were long and his shoulders broad. I have never seen a man like him before or since."

Yet another by the name of Anas ibn Malik said:

"I have never touched silk finer or softer than the palm of the Messenger of Allah's hand; and I have never smelled any scent more fragrant than his natural odour. The Prophet used to visit the sick, attend funerals, travel by donkey and accept the invitation of slaves. The Prophet did not keep anything for himself for the next day. He would give it away for the needy or as charity."

The Prophet's devoted wife A'ishah further said:

"The Prophet spoke slowly and distinctly, pronouncing every word separately so that those who heard him would remember his words. Every night when the Prophet went to bed he would place his palms together, blow upon them and read the protective Surahs: Qulhuwallahu Ahad, Qul A'uzu bi Rabbil-Falaq, and Qul A'uzu bi Rabbin-nas. Then he would rub his hand over his body as far as he could, beginning with his head and face and the front of his body."

His grandson, Hussain, related that his father said that when the Prophet stayed at his house, he divided his time into three parts: he devoted one part to Allah, another for his family, and the remaining part for his *ummah* (and himself).

The Prophet Muhammad disliked gossip, especially the kind that speaks ill of people behind their backs. He was always extra careful in this regard.

When the Prophet walked, he would do so relatively fast-paced, sprightly in his gait, and looking downwards as if against the wind.

"Those who believed before you were mutilated. Their bodies were cut into pieces by iron saws and their flesh torn apart. However, even this torture could not turn them from the truth. By Allah, Islam will one day reign supreme. The day is not very far off when a traveler will go from Sana to Hadralmaut without fear. He will be filled with only the fear of Allah."

Qadi Abu'l-Fadl 'Iyad ibn Musa al-Yahsubi (*circa* 530 AH), was an Imam of his time in *Hadith* and its sciences. He was also a scholar of *Tafsir*, a *Faqih* in *Usul*, as well as a scholar in the battles and lineages of the Arabs. In describing the Prophet "Muhammad, Messenger of Allah, 'Ash-Shifa of Qadi Iyad," he related:

"So what then can be said of the inestimable worth of someone who possesses all of these qualities (of good character: such as practice of the Deen, knowledge, forbearance, patience, thankfulness, justice, doing-without, humility, pardon, chastity, generosity, courage, modesty, manliness, silence, deliberation, gravity, mercy, good manners, and comradeship) in such abundance that they cannot be counted or expressed in words? It would be impossible him to have gained them either by graft or guile. Such a thing is only possible by the gift of Allah the Almighty."
[Preface of book 'Muhammad, Messenger of Allah' in page 32]

Daisaku Ikeda, the spiritual leader of Soka Gakkai International, a worldwide lay Buddhist organization and called by Time Magazine as the 'most powerful man in Japan," in a dialogue with Majid Tehranian, professor of international communication at the University of Hawaii, said of the Prophet of Islam that although "wealthy, conservative people of his time considered him potentially subversive of the established social order, the poor and ordinary people supported him. It is said that he had a large following among young people. The ruling authorities that had first ignored or even ridiculed Muhammad soon found him a force to be reckoned with and began to persecute him and his followers. Over time, it was his personal integrity that rescued him from extreme adversity and provided him with a new setting for activity in Medina. The whole episode shows that his noble character was the great asset that supported him in crisis."

All these leadership qualities are enveloped in the Islamic value system and reflected in the daily life of the Prophet Muhammad.

In the context of modern history, the Prophet of Islam was given a more objective analysis only after the period of the 19th century, by European scholars. They wrote that his contemporaries truly admired him for his courage, resoluteness, impartiality, and for a firmness that was tempered by generosity. He won the hearts of the people by his personal charm. He was gentle, they said, especially with children. Though he was taciturn in nature and sometimes silent in thought, most of the time he was engaged in purposeful endeavours. He became the exemplar of virtuous character, and reports presented him as culturalising the Islamic epitome of human life.

By 622 AD, when the Prophet realised his personal safety was under threat, he prepared to emigrate (embark on the *Hijrah*) to the oasis settlement of Yathrib to accept the allied Ansar's offer of hospitality and protection. In Yathrib, the Prophet Muhammad crafted a new community, comprising an amalgam of Quraishite *Muhajirun* (Arabic: emigrants) and *Ansar* (Arabic: helpers or allies) drawn from the two Arab tribes there. Apart from internal threats, the Prophet's main enemy was from the polytheistic Makkans some 350 kilometres in the south-west. The Messenger of Allah then built the groundwork for an influential Islamic city-state to emerge as the bastion of power.

In early 624 AD a relatively small force of ill-equipped Muslims had defeated a small Makkan army thrice its numerical size, but gave the Prophet Muhammad the first campaign victory at Badr. It bolstered the confidence of the believers that God Almighty was on their side. But a year later, the Prophet almost lost his life when the Makkan force mounted an attack at Uhud. The military reversal was a lesson learned. In 627 AD the Prophet's defence of Madinah survived a prospective attack by Abu Sufyan's confederate force. And by 629 AD, the Prophet of Islam was able to wrest control of Makkah without bloodshed. He magnanimously granted a general amnesty to all its occupants, without the threat of revenge.

In March of 632 AD, the Prophet of Allah undertook his final farewell pilgrimage to Makkah, where he delivered his last sermon (see subsequent text of *Khutbat Al-Wada'*).

The Prophet Muhammad fell ill soon after his return and passed away on 8 June 632 AD in the home of the favourite of his many wives, A'ishah. His last resting place in the main mosque of Madinah is venerated and visited by Muslim pilgrims from all over the world.

THE PROPHET'S FAREWELL SERMON

The Prophet Muhammad bid his final farewell with his *Khutbat al-Wada'* sermon delivered on the 9th of Dzul Hijjah (the 12th and last month of the Islamic year), the 10th year of Hijrah (emigration from Makkah to Madinah) in the Uranah Valley of Mount Arafah. He delivered a simple yet profound message for peace, justice, trustworthiness and felicity for all.

It was a farewell delivery not just to his *ummah* but to all of humanity, for his universal mission as a devoted messenger, a guide to the right path and as a mercy to all believers on earth was almost fully accomplished. He had undertaken his arduous assignment as a vicegerent and messenger of God Almighty in full measure and in good stead, despite the numerous obstacles and tribulations he and his loved ones faced. Over the period of only 23 years as a Prophet and Messenger, he had transformed the whole of his homeland from the throes of ignorance to enlightenment, from backwardness to civilization, from despair to hope. Most of all the Prophet has put us on the straight path from a state of bestial living to the purity of the worship of Allah, the one and only God Almighty.

The Prophet of Islam reminded his followers of the blessedness of life and the sanctity of earning interest-free wealth, all of which are attributable to God's magnanimous compassion to His creations on earth. He asked them not to commit wrongdoings against each other, not to cheat or steal, and not to blood-let because every Muslim is a brother to every Muslim and that all Muslims constitute one brotherhood. He cautioned them not to fall prey to Satan's constant urgings as he has lost all hope that he will be able to lead the good Muslims astray in big things, so the Prophet told them to beware of following him in small things. He reminded them that all Muslims are brothers and that they should treat each other with good intentions.

The Prophet counseled his followers to be mindful of good husband-wife relationships, not to allow the wives to be taken advantage of by evil-minded men, and that the menfolk should always treat their spouses with respect, fairness and dignity.

A cautionary and important prompt by the Prophet to his followers is to constantly abide by the teachings of the Qur'an and the Sunnah, for which in doing so they will never go astray in life.

The final gesture by the Prophet of Islam on Mount Arafah was to look up and ask God the Almighty whether he as the chosen Messenger, has delivered the message.

God Almighty responded by sending down the Qur'anic verse that bore testimony to Prophet Muhammad's eternal legacy on earth:

"This day, I have perfected your religion for you, completed My favour upon you, and have chosen for you Islam as your religion."
[Qur'an, Al-Ma'idah, The Food, 5:3]

The Prophet Muhammad earnestly pleaded with them (his *Ummah*) to dutifully perform the obligatory five daily prayers (*salah*), to fast during the month of Ramadan, to give their wealth in *Zakat*, and to perform the Hajj if they can afford to. He urged the importance of propagating the message of this sermon to all those who are not privy to be at this farewell gathering.

(Khutbat Al-Wada')

"O people, listen to my words. I do not know if I will ever meet with you in this place after this year. O people, your blood and your wealth is sacred until you meet your Lord. You are going to meet your Lord and He will question you about your deeds. Anyone who has a trust, let him return it to the one who entrusted him. Return the goods entrusted to you to their rightful owners. Hurt no one so that no one may hurt you. Allah has forbidden you to take usury (interest). All interest payments are non-valid. For you is the principal of your money. Don't be wrongdoers or the one who is wronged. Allah has enjoined that there is no interest, and the interest of Abbas ibn Abdul Muttalib is all non-valid. All mankind is from Adam and Eve. An Arab has no superiority over a non-Arab, nor has a non-Arab superiority over an Arab. A white has no superiority over a black… (none has superiority over another), except by piety and good-doing. To proceed, O people, Satan has forever given up hope of being worshipped by you in your land, but he is hoping in other than this that while he will not be able to lead you astray in big things, beware of following him in small things concerning your religion. So they made unlawful what Allah made lawful, and what is lawful, unlawful. The number of the months in the sight of Allah is twelve. From them, four are sacred. To proceed, O people, you have rights upon your wives and they have rights upon you. Your right upon them is that they do not let in your bed any who you hate, and it is upon them not to commit an open sin. If they commit a sin, Allah gave you the leave to abandon them in their beds and to hit them mildly. If they refrain from such deeds, it is upon you to supply their maintenance of clothing according to custom. I recommend you to be good to women. You take them as your wives by Allah's trust and with His permission. If they abide by your right, then to them belongs the right to be fed and clothed in kindness. Do treat your women well and be kind to them for they are your partners and committed helpers. And it is your right that they do not make friends with any one of whom you do not approve, and they should never be unchaste. O people, comprehend my speech, because I have delivered, and I have left among you that which if you hold fast to it, you will not go astray. It is a clear affair, Allah's Book and the Sunnah of His Prophet. O people, listen to my speech and comprehend it. Worship Allah, say your five daily prayers, fast during Ramadan, and give your wealth in Zakat. Perform Hajj if you can afford to. You know that every Muslim is a brother to other Muslims and all Muslims are brothers. It is not lawful for one to take anything belonging to his brother, except that which was freely given to him. So, do not be wrongdoers to each other. O people, no prophet or apostle will come after me and no new faith will be born. O Allah, have I delivered (the message)?"

CONCLUSION

Serve to Lead

"On a journey, the lord of a people is their servant" - Muhammad

I have written this guidebook for the love of the Prophet of Islam, and I truly pray that I have done so with the focus it deserves. For all true Muslim believers, it is because of his legacy and total sacrifice that we have been able to prevail as good Muslims throughout the far corners of this earth. It is, therefore, incumbent upon us to continue the altruistic service tradition left by our beloved Prophet to preserve the sanctity of Islam as it was meant to be.

The Prophet Muhammad is the ideal leader held in the highest esteem by Muslims throughout the globe and by many non-Muslims as well. As a leader of distinction and a paragon of excellence, he displayed immense versatility in the many vocations that he pursued: as a shepherd, trader, entrepreneur, military commander, arbitrator, manager-administrator, diplomat, mentor, head of family, religious leader and benevolent proselytiser.

As a leader, the Prophet Muhammad was amiable, a good albeit taciturn communicator, full of patience, and extremely humble. As an action-oriented leader he was hugely courageous, always being on the front-line when it mattered most. He was always sharing himself for the important works that needed to be done.

I would like to elicit three distinctive instances of the Prophet of Islam's main attributes. First: on one occasion, the Prophet was drawing up the Muslim troops in their formations.

"Truly Allah loves those who fight in solid lines for His cause, like a well-compacted wall."

[Qur'an, As-Saff, The Ranks, 61:4]

As the Prophet was pacing up the line straightening it with an arrow in his hand, he faced one Sawadi ibn Ghaziya, who was clearly out of line. The Prophet remarked, "Stand in line, O Sawadi!" while gently pricking him in the stomach with his arrow. With much exaggeration as if in pain, Sawadi cried out, "You have hurt me, O Apostle of God. As God has sent you to teach us about right and justice, please allow me to get even with you. To which the Prophet smilingly obliged by saying, "Here, take your revenge," baring his own belly. Sawadi immediately kissed it and embraced him. Such is the quality of equitable leadership.

Second, in what is a most inspiring episode when analysing the Prophet Muhammad's leadership was when he faced apparent disappointment from some of the ranks of his allies, the Ansar. Word had gone round that the war booties were not distributed equitably enough to the Ansar helpers who had fought side-by-side, through thick-and-thin with him in the military campaigns. It was felt that they had not got the share of camels, while other Makkans and chieftains from the desert nomadic tribes who had just embraced Islam received generous offerings. Sa'ad ibn Ubada, the chief of one of the two Ansar tribes, in honesty told the Prophet what was being said among the ranks. As usual, the Prophet Muhammad, wanted feedback and asked Sa'ad what his personal feeling was on the matter. Sa'ad said he concurred with his men. The Prophet reflected, and then asked Sa'ad to rally his men so that he could personally address them. He started off by saying:

"O Helpers. What is this that I hear of you? Do you think ill of me in your hearts? Did I not come to you when you were erring and God guided you; poor and God made you rich; enemies and God softened your hearts?

Why don't you answer me? Does generosity only belong to God and his Messenger? [*pause*]

Had you so wished, you could have said (to me): 'You came to us discredited, and we believed in you; deserted and we helped you; a fugitive and we took you in; poor and we comforted you.'

In saying this, you would have spoken the truth.

[*pause*]

Are you disturbed in your minds because of the good things of this life by which I win over a people that they may become Muslims, while I entrust you to your reliance upon God?

Are you not satisfied that other men should take away flocks and herds, while you take the Messenger of God back with you to Madinah? If all men went one way and the Helpers the other, that I should take the way of the Helpers. May God have mercy on the Helpers, their sons and their sons' sons!"

The Prophet's impacting speech reminds one of the famous speech delivered by Mark Antony (a close companion of Julius Caesar): "Friends, Romans, and Countrymen...Lend me your ears!"

The Prophet's short address was so moving that the Ansar shed tears of joy for the Messenger of Allah's total commitment to them; but having initially taken the Prophet for granted, they felt so ashamed of themselves. Such is quality of inspirational leadership.

A third episode attributed to the Prophet concerned his integrity as a leader of substance. In 622 AD, the Prophet made plans to trek peacefully to Makkah for a 3-day pilgrimage. With some 1,000 devout followers, carrying swords (but not bows or lances), he set out to march southward. However, the Quraish were bent on preventing the believers from entering the vicinity of the Ka'abah.

Negotiations to enter Makkah broke down, but a 10-year truce was meted out, that in the view of his followers (especially his principal companion Umar), was not to the Muslims' advantage. God knows best.

As soon as the Quraish envoys had left the valley of Hudaibiyyah where they had met, the Prophet decided to sacrifice the 70 garlanded camels they had brought along with them for the Makkan rites at the Ka'abah, to be sacrificed there and then. It was like a simulation event, conducted in the Hudaibiyyah campsite rather than at the Ka'abah. When the Prophet commanded, "Rise and sacrifice your animals and shave your heads," the followers remained still, displaying their unhappiness that their objective to be in Makkah had not materialised.

The Prophet commanded them three times, yet they remained unmoved.

The Prophet was sad, and entered his tent somewhat disconsolate. It so happened that one of his wives, Umm Salamah, had accompanied him on this trip. In the tent, she advised the Prophet to go out again and without saying anything advised him to perform the rites himself in front of his followers.

So he went down again into the valley, approached his garlanded personal camel, and in the name of Allah the Merciful, sacrificed it. The Muslim followers who witnessed the spectacle were overawed. And then, as if by instinct, all of them followed suit. The crisis of confidence was over. Such is the power of leadership by example.

The chapters in the guidebook serve to briefly explain the roles played by the Prophet of Islam in the transformation process. Beginning with the core Altruistic Service Leadership (ASL) Model, embracing the 3+4+5 = Felicity through the Synergy framework, I have proceeded to analyse the *Economic Leader, Social Master* profile of the Prophet of Islam. The Prophet's early experience in his youth as a competent trading caravan head with its attendant risk-taking activities, his responsibility for the entire band of people and their assets, and the trust placed upon him to look after their wellbeing on several expeditions tested his mettle. His ability to manage and administer his portfolio as head of government in Madinah guided by his Constitution of Madinah which promoted a series of far-reaching economic and social reforms, along with his diplomatic forays outside of the Arabian Peninsula showed that his overall competencies point to a 9,9 one-best style team leadership orientation.

As a transformational leader, the seven-step process of how the Prophet managed the progression of change was the forerunner to the establishment of the Islamic city-state that has weathered the test of time. As a family man right up to the level of an international statesman, the Prophet of Islam has shown by example that he is the most ideal yet humble leader to be emulated by all.

> *"The true servants of the Most Gracious God are those who walk on earth with humility, and when the ignorant address them (harshly), they say (words of) 'Peace!'"*
> [Qur'an, Al-Furqan, The Criterion, 25:63]

Prophet Muhammad's leadership model narrated in this guidebook which is well-researched, extensively field-tested, with its analysis-based feedback, is pragmatic for the promising leader of substance.

May Allah continue to bless all who follow in his revered footsteps.

ABOUT THE AUTHOR

ISMAIL NOOR first learned about leadership when he studied for several years at the Royal Military College, Malaysia's version of the Royal Military Academy Sandhurst in Britain. After attaining his basic degree in history at the country's premier University of Malaya in Kuala Lumpur, he undertook post-graduate studies in management in the United States. Thereafter he set up a human resource training centre in Kuala Lumpur, at which many thousand aspirants in Malaysia and the Southeast Asian region have attended his flagship altruistic leadership course based on the Prophet of Islam's model. Participants included representatives from several government ministries/departments/

agencies, corporate entities, academic institutions and non-governmental organizations.

Ismail has written, edited and self-published some 30 books on the subjects of leadership, management and total quality which led to the country's national library naming him a 'prolific writer'. This book is his first attempt to go global. He has travelled widely and sat on the board of several companies and training institutions in the country. He has been appointed an international Peace Ambassador by the Universal Peace Federation (UPF), which has special consultative status with the Economic & Social Council (ECOSOC) of the United Nations (UN).

BIBLIOGRAPHY

Books

- Abdul Hamid A. Abu Sulayman, "Towards an Islamic Theory of International Relations: New Directions for Methodology and Thought," Islamic Knowledge Series (1), International Institute of Islamic Thought, Herndon, Virginia, USA, 1993.
- Adair, John Eric, "THE ACTION-CENTRED LEADER," The Industrial Society, U.K., 1998.
- Adair, John Eric, "The Leadership of MUHAMMAD," Kogan Page, London, 2010.
- Afzalur Rahman (Editor), "MUHAMMAD – Encyclopaedia of Seerah," Volumes I – VII, Seerah Foundation, London, 1986.
- Akbar Ahmed, "JOURNEY INTO ISLAM – The Crisis of Globalization," Brrokings Institution Press, Washington DC., 2007.
- Ahmad Von Denffer, "A DAY WITH THE PROPHET," THE ISLAMIC FOUNDATION, UK., International Islamic Publishing House, Saudi Arabian Edition, 2008
- Akram Diya' al-Umari, "Madinan Society at the Time of the Prophet," Vols. I & II, International Institute of Islamic Thought, Virginia, USA, 1991.
- Brigadier (Retd.) Gulzar Ahmad, "THE BATTLES OF THE PROPHET OF ALLAH," Vols. I & II, Islamic Publications (Private) Limited, Lahore, Pakistan, 1985-1986.
- Campbell, Andrew; Devine, Marion; Young, David; "A Sense of Mission," – Ashridge, The Economist Books, Hutchinson, London, 1990.
- Cashman, Kevin, "Awakening the Leader Within – A Story of Transformation," John Wiley & Sons Inc., New Jersey, USA, 2003.
- Golan W. Choudhury, "THE PROPHET MUHAMMAD – His Life and Eternal Message," WHS Publications Sdn Bhd., Kuala Lumpur, 1993.

- Gabriel, Richard A., "MUHAMMAD – ISLAM'S FIRST GREAT GENERAL," University of Oklahoma Press, Norman, USA, 2007.
- Hart, Michael H., "The 100 – A Ranking of the Most Influential Persons in History," Carol Publishing Group/Citadel Press, New York, 1992.
- Harvard Business Review, "Ethics for Executives: Part I," Harvard College, USA, 1970.
- Ikeda, Daisaku & Tehranian, Majid., "GLOBAL CIVILIZATION, A Buddhist-Islamic Dialogue," British Academic Press, London, 2003.
- Iqbal Ahmad Azami, "MUHAMMAD the Beloved Prophet – A Great Story Simply Told," UK Islamic Academy, Leicester, U.K., 1994.
- Ismail Noor, "PROPHET MUHAMMAD'S LEADERSHIP – The Paragon of Excellence," Utusan Publications & Distributors Sdn Bhd, 2002.
- Lennick, Doug & Kiel, Fred, "Moral Intelligence – Enhancing Business Performance & Leadership Success," Wharton School Publishing, New Jersey, 2005.
- Matsushita, Konosuke, "THOUGHTS ON MAN," PHP Institute International, Inc., Tokyo, 1982.
- Mohd Kamal Hassan, "VOICE OF ISLAMIC MODERATION FROM THE MALAY WORLD," Emerging Markets Innovative Research, EMIR, Ipoh, Perak, Malaysia, 2011.
- Muhammad Ali al-Hashimi, "THE IDEAL MUSLIM – The True Personality as Defined in the Qur'an and Sunnah," International Islamic Publishing House, Riyadh, Saudi Arabia, 1997.
- Muhammad Siddique Qureshi, Prof. "Foreign Policy of Hadrat Muhammad Sallallahu Alaihi Wassalam," Kitab Bhavan, New Delhi, India, 1991.
- Muhammad Taqi-ud-Din Al-Hilali & Muhammad Muhsin Khan, "The Noble Qur'an," Darussalam Publishers & Distributors, Riyadh, 1996.
- Qadi 'Iyad ibn Musa al-Yahsubi, "Muhammad – Messenger of Allah, Ash-Shifa of Qadi 'Iyad," Madinah Press, Granada, Spain, 1992.
- Reg Hamilton, "A Practical Guide to the Skills of Mentoring," The Industrial Society, Pelanduk Publications, 1996.
- Saba Islamic Media, "Know this Man," Kuala Lumpur (undated).
- Saiyid Sulaiman Nadwi, "MUHAMMAD THE IDEAL PROPHET - A Historical, Practical, Perfect Model for Humanity," Islamic Book Trust, Kuala Lumpur, 1977.

- Siddiqui, A.H., "The Life of MUHAMMAD," published by S. Sajid Ali, Adam Publishers & Distributors, Delhi, India, 1994.
- Sliman Ben Ibrahim and Etienne Dinet, "THE LIFE OF MOHAMMAD – PROPHET OF ALLAH," Chartwell Books, Inc., 1990.
- Sulaiman Ibn 'Awad Qaiman, "SECRETS OF LEADERSHIP AND INFLUENCE, Dakwah Corner Bookstore, 2010.
- Syed Muhammad Naquib al-Attas and Wan Mohd. Nor bin Wan Daud," The ICLIF Leadership Competency Model (LCM): An Islamic Alternative," ICLIF, Kuala Lumpur, 2007.
- Vogel, David, "The Market for Virtue – The Potential and Limits of Corporate Social Responsibility," Brookings Institution Press, Washington D.C., 2005.
- Ziauddin Kirmani, "THE LAST MESSENGER WITH A LASTING MESSAGE – An Unconventional Study," Taj Company, New Delhi, 1983.
- Ziauddin Sardar, "MUHAMMAD: Aspects of His Biography," The Islamic Foundation, Leicester, U.K., 1992.

Articles

- Cole, Bill, "The Art of Team Building: Leaders can achieve their organizational goals by grooming strong teams," Star Metro, Saturday 3 April, 2010.
- Mohamed Iqbal, Chairman Malaysian Institute of Management, "Leader of a people is their servant," New Sunday Times, Sunday 5 February, 2012.
- Mohammad Hashim Kamali, CEO IAIS Malaysia" What Makes the Muslim Leader," New Straits Times, Comment, p.16, Monday, May 31, 2010.
- Mohd Farid Mohd Shahran, PhD, Director of Ikim's Centre for Study of Shariah, Law and Politics, "Trusting the Power of Leadership," Ikim's Views, The Star, Tuesday 28 July 2015.
- Roshan Thiran, CEO Leaderonomics, "Building high performance teams – leadership lessons from the 'Special One'," The Star, Starbizweek, Viewpoints, Saturday 21 August, 2010.

GLOSSARY

'abd	: Slave or servant of Allah the Almighty
Adab-al-Ikhtilaf	: Having the required respect and tolerance and understanding of differences among human beings or scholars
Al-'adalah	: Justice
Akhirah	: The Hereafter (eternal life) which starts from the Day of Resurrection, when all human beings are restored to life to face the Judgment of Allah Almighty
akhlaq	: Morality, ethics, the practice of virtue, or God-given principles of good-doing
amanah	: Trust
amr ma'ruf nahy munkar	: The Qur'anic injunction of enjoining good, prohibiting evil
al-ananiyyah	: Egotism and selfishness, an attitude that is concerned mainly with one's personal gain or pleasure at the expense of others
anfa' al-nas	: The most helpful person to others
Ansar	: Literally means "supporters," the early Muslims of Madinah who welcomed and assisted the Migrants from Makkah, who were continually persecuted and harassed by the Makkan polytheists.

al-'aql	: Intellect, intelligence or reason
ayat	: Verses of the Qur'an, signs and revelations of Allah, God Almighty
ayat Allah	: Signs of God Almighty in man, society, history, civilization, nature, animals and the universe
bai'ah	: Pledge of allegiance to the leader
bid'ah	: Innovation in religious matters
al-baghy	: Various kinds of oppression; causing others to feel down-trodden, overwhelmed by those in power
barakah	: Blessings, favours or grace given by God Almighty
dakwah	: Duty to propagate Islam to the whole of mankind
Din	: Religion of belief system constituting the way of life
Din al-rahmah	: Islam as a religion of peace, compassion and mercy
dunya	: The present world, as opposed to the Hereafter, as a transient abode of mankind and a prelude to the everlasting life
fahsha'(al-fahsha')	: Evil deeds and obscenities, viewed as offensive and disgusting by the Islamic code of conduct

fard 'ain	: Religious obligation incumbent upon every individual Muslim, e.g. 5 daily prayers, fasting during Ramadan, etc
fard kifayah	: Religious obligation upon the whole Muslim community, like someone respectfully burying the dead.
fi'l al-khair	: Performing socially beneficial work
fikr al-wasati	: Islamic moderation thought; justly-balanced thinking
Fiqh	: Islamic jurisprudence
fitrah	: The good, innate spiritual nature of man, as created by God
Hadith	: Words, sayings or deeds of Prophet Muhammad; prophetic Tradition
halal	: Permissible or good for consumption
haram	: Unlawful and forbidden
hikmah	: Wisdom or sound judgement
huquq al-insan	: Human rights
hurriyyah	: Freedom
'ibadah	: Worship of or servanthood to God Almighty
ifrat	: Immoderation and excessiveness
Ihsan	: Benevolence, good-doing for the sake of God Almighty

ijab bi al-nafs	: Vanity; self-conceited for one's own special qualities
ijtihad	: Independent reasoning or the making of a ruling in Islamic law by personal or group effort, as opposed to *taqlid* (imitation)
Ikhtilaf	: Plurality or differences of opinion
Imam	: Mosque or prayer leader, or a leader in general
iman	: Faith or belief
infitah, al-infitah	: Openness and acceptance of other opinions based on mutual respect, without coercion
insaf	: Being fair and just
Injil	: The original divine scripture revealed by God Almighty to Jesus (the Prophet Isa *a.s.*)
al-intilaq	: Inclusivism
al-inhilaq	: Exclusivism and dogmatism, by firmly asserting one's personal or group opinion as the only true opinion
al-Islam al-Siyasi	: Political Islam, or political aspects of Islam's worldview, dealing with state formation, governance and politics
al-istiqamah	: Straightness and constancy of purpose, being truly committed to a particular cause
I'tiqad	: Faith or creed, one's firm belief in something
Iqra'	: Read! Or Recite! The first revealed word of the Qur'an

Islah	: Reform, promotion of peace, world order, wellbeing or good relationships
istidlal	: Reasoning and inference, arriving at conclusions by evidence and reasoning
itqan	: The search for quality or excellence
Jahiliyyah	: Relating to the period of ignorance, particularly during the Pre-Islamic period in the Arabian Peninsula
Jihad	: Striving or exerting sincere effort to achieve a spiritual goal
Khalifah	: Man as vicegerent holding God Almighty's trust or duty on earth to fulfill His commandments
al-khuluq al-Qurani	: Quranic morality, a set of behavior conforming to the values and principles enjoined by the divine, holy book
al-lin	: Tenderness and friendliness, not being crude or rough
ma'ruf	: A good deed, approved practice or the right action
maddiyyah	: Materialism, material possessions and physical comfort as superior to spiritual values
madhhab	: An Islamic school of thought or jurisprudence, as in Shafie, Hanafi, Maliki or Hanbali
maghfirah	: Forgiveness

mal Allah	: The property of Allah, which includes everything in the universe
manhaj	: Methodology or approach
Mu'min	: Muslim believer, subscribing to the Oneness of Allah
mufsidun	: Those who commit crime and sin, oppressors, mischief-makers and corrupters
Muhajirun	: The early Muslim migrants who migrated to Madinah
muhsinin	: Good-doers
mushrikun	: Polytheists, idolaters, pagans, disbelievers in the Oneness of Allah
qisas	: Punishment by retaliation, part of Islamic criminal law
qital	: Physical fighting, battle or killing
Rabb (al-Alamin)	: God Almighty, Lord and Sustainer of the Universe
riba	: Interest or usury, forbidden in Islam
sabr	: Patience and perseverance, obligatory for Muslims
Shari'ah	: The Divine path, the code of life, the Divine Law that Allah has revealed to human beings via His messengers to guide mankind to wellbeing on earth and salvation in the Hereafter. In a practical sense, it refers to

	the Divine Law based on the Qur'an and the norms of the Prophet
Shahadah	: The Testimony of Faith
Shura	: The principle of consensus-seeking consultation by the ruler, the boss, the manager, the leader or by the team itself.
Sunnah	: The *Sunnah*, after the Qur'an, is the second most authoritative source of knowledge in Islamic teachings. Specifically it refers to the sayings and deeds of the Prophet Muhammad *s.a.w* as recorded in the *Hadith* which is regarded as having legally binding precedents
taqwa	: God-consciousness, which implies fear of attaining His displeasure. Aspiring for His pleasure by strictly following His commandments and abiding by His prohibitions
al-tarbiyah wa al-takwin	: Education and character development
tasawwuf	: Sufism, the branch of Islamic religious knowledge and discipline that focuses on man's spiritual relationship with God Almighty
ukhuwwah Islamiyyah	: Islamic brotherhood worldwide based on Islamic faith
ummah	: The universal Muslim community or nation

Ummatan wasatan	: A community in good balance between justice and goodness, which is the position prescribed in the Qur'an (Q2:143)
zalim	: Wrong-doer or unjust person who commits injustice by disobeying the commandments of God Almighty

Index

S

T

Z

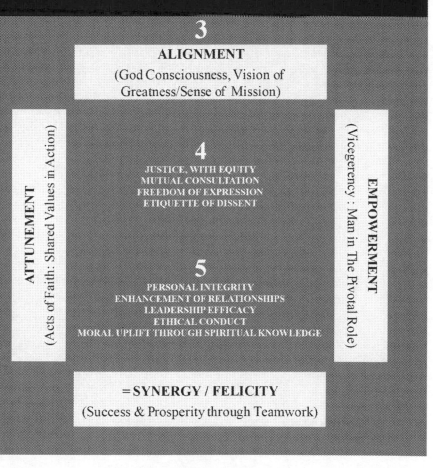

Altruistic Service Leadership
3 Dimensions + 4 Postures + 5 Tenets

3

ALIGNMENT
(God Consciousness, Vision of
Greatness/Sense of Mission)

ATTUNEMENT
(Acts of Faith: Shared Values in Action)

EMPOWERMENT
(Vicegerency: Man in The Pivotal Role)

4

JUSTICE, WITH EQUITY
MUTUAL CONSULTATION
FREEDOM OF EXPRESSION
ETIQUETTE OF DISSENT

5

PERSONAL INTEGRITY
ENHANCEMENT OF RELATIONSHIPS
LEADERSHIP EFFICACY
ETHICAL CONDUCT
MORAL UPLIFT THROUGH SPIRITUAL KNOWLEDGE

= SYNERGY / FELICITY
(Success & Prosperity through Teamwork)

© Ismail Noor, PhD

*"If greatness of purpose, smallness of means, and astounding
results are the criteria of human genius, who could dare to
compare any great man in modern history with Muhammad?"*
– Alphonse de Lamartine (French statesman/poet).

Printed in the United States
By Bookmasters